The SUPER
Achievers

The Remarkable Jewish Contribution to Science and Human Well-being Highlighted by Nobel Prize Winners

Ronald Ge

The vastly disproportionate number of Jewish Nobel Prize winners in medicine and science exemplifies Jewish achievement and contributions to knowledge and human well-being.

With only 0.2% of the world's population, Jews have been awarded 24% of the Nobel Prizes in medicine and science. American Jews, who account for 2% of all Americans, have received 37% of U.S. awards.

ISBNs
Hardcover: 978-0-578-54946-0
Softcover: 978-0-578-62922-3

Published by
Excelsis Press

Editor: Erica Rauzin

Cover and interior design: Gary A. Rosenberg
www.thebookcouple.com

Cover photo reprinted with permission of Sipa Press.

Printed in the United States of America

In memory and appreciation of my parents,
Egon Gerstl & Georgie Gerö Gerstl

To the super achievers—
all the scientists and medical doctors
who have contributed so much to human knowledge
and well-being—most of whom are unknown
to the general public.

*"Aim high because you can always fall back,
but if you aim low there is nothing to fall back to."*

—LEON LEDERMAN, Nobel Prize in Physics 1988
(Biography, American Academy of Achievement)

Contents

Selected Biographical Profiles of Jewish Nobel Prizewinners in Medicine, Physics, and Chemistry

Travail & Elation

This book has had a very long gestation period. Unlike most books, this one began by gathering data, which led to writing about the surprising findings. The result is *The Super Achievers*. Much has been written about this subject but the information is scattered and fragmented. The list of Jewish Nobel prizewinners in the sciences mentioned herein is likely the most comprehensive of its kind. The book brings disparate information together in an interesting and interpretative manner. It adds perspective on the accomplishments of Jewish laureates within the broader context of human intelligence and achievement worldwide.

The Super Achievers is purposefully compact, which should appeal to readers who may be turned off by long, plodding, and overly scholarly works. Each chapter, by itself, has enough material to fill a book. Hopefully it will awaken interest and encourage further reading. Many of these scientists' lives embody the universal themes of resilience and triumph over adversity. You don't have to be Jewish to find interesting such topics as the rarified world of the Nobel Prizes, the lives and discoveries of ground-breaking scientists, how America benefitted from the scientists who fled Nazi Germany, achievement around the globe, women science Nobelists, and science versus religion.

Personally, I believe that there has not been sufficient awareness and recognition of Jews' disproportionately large contributions to knowledge and human well-being. Jews are usually not characterized as a modest people. In reality, however, Jews have been somewhat reticent to tout their achievements. Two thousand years of persecution and exclusion have been an effective inhibitor to braggadocio. Some readers of this book—and probably even those who have not read it—may deem *The Super Achievers* boastful and/or politically incorrect. However, the contents are based on data backed up by exhibits.

I would like this book to reach a broad readership, not only Jews. In some modest way, I hope it may contribute to the appreciation of the amazing role that Jews have played in America and the world. Unlike so many books that by necessity are concerned with past Jewish suffering, *The Super Achievers* is an upbeat chronicle of accomplishment and resilience. It should be a source of pride to Jews, no matter how little how or how much they personally identify with the religion.

Although I have diligently researched the material over many years, I recognize that inevitably there may be some unintentional errors, for which I apologize beforehand and welcome corrections. If there is another edition, I will be pleased to rectify them.

Readers Please Note

- For the sake of brevity throughout the book we refer to the official Nobel Prize award designation of **Physiology and Medicine** simply as "**Medicine**."

- At the author's behest, "**prizewinners**" is written as one word and "**antisemitism**" is written without the traditional hyphen and a capital "S."

- "**Honorand**" is Nobel-speak for a Nobel prizewinner (laureate). "**Nobelist**" is also sometimes used.

- An asterisk (*) after the name of a Nobel laureate indicates that there is a **biographical profile** later in the book.

- Upper case, **superscript** M, P, or C after a laureate's name indicates that additional data is available in Exhibits I, III, and IV.

I. The Super Achievers

"Properly, the Jew ought hardly to be heard of; but he is heard of, has always been heard of... His contributions to the world's list of great names in literature, science, art, music, finance, medicine, and abstruse learning are also way out of proportion to the weakness of his numbers. He has made a marvelous fight in this world, in all the ages; and has done it with his hands tied behind him. He could be vain of himself, and be excused for it."[1]

—MARK TWAIN

As so quaintly stated by Mark Twain, Jews ought hardly to be heard of, but are always heard of, and some might say heard of too much. Even Mark Twain would have to be surprised that with only 0.2% of the world's population, Jews have been awarded 24% of all Nobel Prizes in science and medicine. With only 2% of the U.S. population, American Jews have received 37% of American awards.

Why are there so many Jewish achievers? After all, Jews constitute only a tiny minority of the population. Curious about this observation, I started by jotting down names of musicians and composers,

---

1 *Concerning the Jew,* Harper & Bros., New York, 1934, p. 23

outstanding leaders in industry and finance, inventors and scientists. As the list grew, the idea of a book took root. Should I write about business titans who helped forge America's financial and industrial might? Should I concentrate on contributions to music? To cover all areas of Jewish achievement would require multiple volumes. Just to write about the works of stellar composers of the American musical theatre, such as Jerome Kern, Irving Berlin, George Gershwin, Richard Rodgers, and Leonard Bernstein—to name just a few— would necessitate a book by itself. They created a uniquely American art form that has become part of the fabric of American life.

Unlike other fields of human endeavor, such as the arts or literature, which are by necessity often evaluated by subjective criteria, achievements in science can be evaluated with a high degree of objectivity. What's more, there exists a universally recognized measure—the Nobel Prize—the world's most prestigious award and the highest distinction that can be bestowed for scientific merit. Consequently, the book focuses on Jewish Nobel prize-winners in the sciences—medicine, physics and chemistry—even though personally I am far more familiar with the worlds of business and music.

Except for scientists and academicians, most of us, at best, have heard of only a few Nobel science laureates. This is an unfortunate reflection of our society. While most people are obsessed with professional athletes, and movie and television personalities, they hardly know or care about outstanding scientists who have made a difference. How many kids do you know who collect famous scientist cards? Einstein and Jonas Salk can hardly compete with such celebrities as Mickey Mantle and Elvis Presley.

Contributions by Jews to the scientific and cultural development of the world, in general, and of the United States, in particular, have been vastly out of proportion to their number. By any measure, whether based on demographics or probability theory, it is amazing that such a small segment of the population has achieved so much. Jews constitute a tiny fraction of the world's population, just 0.2 percent. A workable estimate is 15.8 million (Jewish demographics are discussed in Chapter VI), less than one-fifth of one percent of the Earth's inhabitants. More people live in Mexico City, Cairo, or Seoul than there are Jews in the world. There are seventeen times more Indonesians and thirteen times more Nigerians.

In the 118 years from 1901—when the Nobel Prizes were first awarded—through 2018, there have been 607 award recipients for medicine, physics and chemistry. Of these prizewinners, 24%—nearly one out of four—is of Jewish origin (the complete list appears in Exhibit I following this chapter). If the prizes had been awarded on a proportionate basis, Jews should have earned only one or two. Instead, there have been 148 Jewish Nobel science prizewinners—a startling over-representation of more than 120 times of what could be expected statistically.

From an American perspective, Jewish representation is even greater. Through 2018, Americans garnered 275 Nobel science prizes, 45% of the world total, more than any other nation. The American recipients include 101 Jews, 37% of all U.S. awards (see Exhibit II). Since Jews comprise about 2% of the U.S. population, Jewish American laureates are over represented among U.S. Nobel science prizewinners by a factor of 19 times.

Viewed by categories (see Exhibit III), Jewish achievement has been particularly noteworthy in medicine, with 41% of all U.S. Nobel Prize awards in that field, followed closely by physics with 40%. Jews may be best known for their contributions to medicine. Their discoveries and innovations—frequently made jointly with non-Jewish colleagues—resulted in life-saving drugs, discoveries and procedures that have benefited mankind.

discovery of the two families of proteins which regulate them, the G protein-coupled receptor kinases and beta-arrestins."[3] One cannot help but feel perplexed trying to understand the significance of these discoveries.

The book is primarily concerned with Jewish Nobel science laureates' family and socioeconomic backgrounds, national and ethnic origins (see Chapter IV: "Laureates' National and Ethnic Backgrounds") and their education (see Chapter IX: "Laureates' University Affiliations"). Many of the early laureates led colorful, tumultuous lives and struggled against great odds. With the rise of Nazism, Jewish laureates and laureates-to-be had to flee Europe (see Chapter V. Germany's Loss, America's Gain). The lives of those laureates who came of age before the Second World War were often complex and full of unexpected twists and turns.

Fritz Haber, Captain, German army, World War I

Such was the life of Fritz Haber* (Chemistry 1918) who discovered the way to synthesize ammonia to produce fertilizer, thereby greatly increasing food production, which benefited mankind. But he also was the inventor of poisonous gas and a proponent of chemical warfare. In World War I Germany used the banned poisonous gases resulting in some 150,000 Allied casualties in the battle of Ypres, Belgium.

---

3. Albany Medical Center News Service. "Pioneers of cell receptor research share America's top prize in medicine."

While he was hailed as a hero in Germany, scientists worldwide abhorred his work, and caused his chemist wife to commit suicide. Despite of his services to Germany, he found it necessary to leave for England in 1933. He died shortly thereafter on his way to Tel Aviv to take up a post with the precursor of the Weizmann Institute. Tragically during the Holocaust the Nazis used a formulation of his poisonous gas, Zyklon B, in the gas chambers of the extermination camps.

Some of the earlier scientists suffered life-threatening illnesses or worse as a result of their work. While working on his experiments Henri Moissan* (Chemistry 1906) suffered from exposure to toxic fluoride chemicals, which eventually led to his death. Paul Ehrlich* (Medicine 1908) contracted tuberculosis while performing tests in his laboratory and had to spend two years recovering in Egypt. Charles Gerhardt, who conducted pioneer work on acetylsalicylic acid (aspirin), was poisoned. Some were lucky. Waldemar Haffkine, who developed the vaccine for cholera and bubonic plague, took great risks by testing it on himself without adverse effects.

Waldemar Haffkine

More recent laureates led more conventional lives that usually did not involve the personal and professional struggles of their European pre-World War II predecessors. They frequently conducted research and made their discoveries collaboratively with fellow scientists and in institutional settings, which is also reflected in the trends in awarding Nobel prizes in the sciences. More recent awards are usually shared among two or even three winners, whereas in the earlier years, sole winners were more common.

Lest we think of Jewish achievements in science only in terms of academia and abstruse thinking, note the many Jewish tech entrepreneurs who founded cutting-edge technology companies that have profoundly changed the way we live and work. To cite some of the best known: Michael Dell (Dell), Andrew Grove (Intel), Steve Balmer (Microsoft), Larry Ellison (Oracle), Sergey Brin and Larry Page (Google), and Mark Zuckerberg (Facebook).

Google founders Sergey Brin and Larry Page (left)

While every nation, ethnic group, race, and religion has super achievers, Jews for whatever reasons (explored in Chapter XI. Why the Exceptionalism?) have a higher incidence. It takes someone like Charles Murray, a self-described "Scots-Irish gentile from

Iowa," a Harvard professor and the co-author of *The Bell Curve* (a major research study examining intelligence in America) to note, "the extravagant over representation of Jews relative to their numbers in the top ranks of the arts, sciences, law, medicine, finance, entrepreneurship, and the media...constitutes a fascinating and important story."[4]

4. Murray, Charles. "Jewish Genius." *Commentary,* 1 April 2007

EXHIBIT I
JEWISH NOBEL PRIZEWINNERS IN
MEDICINE, PHYSICS, AND CHEMISTRY

(m) Jewish mother   (f) Jewish father   (3) Three Jewish grandparents

Last Name, First Name	Nobel Prize	Year of Award	Born–Died
Abrikosov, Alexei (m)	Physics	2003	1928–2017
Alferov, Zhores (m)	Physics	2000	1930
Altman, Sidney	Chemistry	1989	1939
Ashkin, Arthur	Physics	2018	1922
Axel, Richard	Medicine	2004	1946
Axelrod, Julius	Medicine	1970	1912–2004
Baeyer, Adolph von (m)	Chemistry	1905	1835–1917
Baltimore, David	Medicine	1975	1938
Barany, Robert	Medicine	1914	1876–1936
Barish, Barry	Physics	2017	1936
Benacerraf, Baruj	Medicine	1980	1920–2011
Berg, Paul	Chemistry	1980	1926
Bethe, Hans (m)	Physics	1967	1906–2005
Beutler, Bruce	Medicine	2011	1957
Bloch, Felix	Physics	1952	1905–1983
Bloch, Konrad	Medicine	1964	1912–2000
Blumberg, Baruch	Medicine	1976	1925–2011
Bohr, Niels (m)	Physics	1922	1885–1962
Born, Max (m)	Physics	1954	1882–1970

Last Name, First Name	Nobel Prize	Year of Award	Born–Died
Brenner, Sydney	Medicine	2002	1927–2019
Brown, Herbert	Chemistry	1979	1912–2004
Brown, Michael	Medicine	1985	1941
Calvin, Melvin	Chemistry	1961	1911–1997
Chain, Sir Ernst	Medicine	1945	1906–1979
Chalfie, Martin	Chemistry	2008	1947
Charpak, Georges	Physics	1992	1924–2010
Ciechanover, Aaron	Chemistry	2004	1947
Cohen, Stanley	Medicine	1986	1922
Cohen-Tannoudji, Claude	Physics	1997	1933
Cooper, Leon	Physics	1972	1930
Cori, Gerty Radnitz	Medicine	1947	1896–1957
Edelman, Gerald	Medicine	1972	1929–2014
Ehrlich, Paul	Medicine	1908	1854–1915
Einstein, Albert	Physics	1921	1879–1955
Elion, Gertrude	Medicine	1988	1918–1999
Englert, Francois	Physics	2013	1932
Erlanger, Joseph	Medicine	1944	1874–1965
Feynman, Richard	Physics	1965	1918–1988
Fire, Andrew	Medicine	2006	1959
Fischer, Edmond (f)	Medicine	1992	1920
Franck, James	Physics	1925	1882–1964
Frank, Ilya (f)	Physics	1958	1908–1990
Friedman, Jerome	Physics	1990	1930
Furchgott, Robert	Medicine	1998	1916–2009
Gabor, Dennis	Physics	1971	1900–1979

Last Name, First Name	Nobel Prize	Year of Award	Born–Died
Gasser, Herbert (f)	Medicine	1944	1888–1963
Gell-Mann, Murray	Physics	1969	1929–2019
Gilbert, Walter	Chemistry	1980	1932
Gilman, Alfred	Medicine	1994	1941
Ginzburg, Vitaly	Physics	2003	1916–2009
Glaser, Donald	Physics	1960	1926–2013
Glashow, Sheldon	Physics	1979	1932
Glauber, Roy	Physics	2005	1925–2018
Goldstein, Joseph	Medicine	1985	1940
Greengard, Paul (3)	Medicine	2000	1925–2019
Gross, David	Physics	2004	1941
Haber, Fritz	Chemistry	1918	1868–1934
Haroche, Serge	Chemistry	2012	1943
Hauptman, Herbert	Chemistry	1985	1917–2011
Heeger, Alan	Chemistry	2000	1936
Hersko, Avram	Chemistry	2004	1937
Hertz, Gustav (f)	Physics	1925	1887–1975
Hevesy, George de	Chemistry	1943	1885–1966
Hoffmann, Roald	Chemistry	1981	1937
Hofstadter, Robert	Physics	1961	1915–1990
Horvitz, H. Robert	Medicine	2002	1947
Jacob, Francois	Medicine	1965	1920–2012
Josephson, Brian	Physics	1973	1940
Kandel, Eric	Medicine	2000	1929
Kapitsa, Pyotr (m)	Physics	1978	1898–1984
Karle, Jerome	Chemistry	1985	1918–2013

Last Name, First Name	Nobel Prize	Year of Award	Born–Died
Karplus, Martin	Chemistry	2013	1930
Katz, Sir Bernard	Medicine	1970	1911–2003
Klug, Sir Aaron	Chemistry	1982	1926–2018
Kohn, Walter	Chemistry	1998	1923–2016
Kornberg, Arthur	Medicine	1959	1918–2007
Kornberg, Roger	Chemistry	2006	1947
Kosterlitz, J. Michael	Physics	2016	1943
Krebs, Sir Hans	Medicine	1953	1900–1981
Kroto, Sir Harold (f)	Chemistry	1996	1939–2016
Landau, Lev	Physics	1962	1908–1968
Landsteiner, Karl	Medicine	1930	1868–1943
Lederberg, Joshua	Medicine	1958	1925–2008
Lederman, Leon	Physics	1988	1922–2018
Lee, David	Physics	1996	1931
Lefkowitz, Robert	Physics	2012	1943
Levi-Montalcini, Rita	Medicine	1986	1909–2012
Levitt, Michael	Chemistry	2013	1947
Lipmann, Fritz	Medicine	1953	1899–1986
Lippmann, Gabriel	Physics	1908	1845–1921
Loewi, Otto	Medicine	1936	1873–1961
Luria, Salvador	Medicine	1969	1912–1991
Lwoff, Andre	Medicine	1965	1902–1994
Marcus, Rudolph	Chemistry	1992	1923
Metchnikoff, Ilya (m)	Medicine	1908	1845–1916
Meyerhof, Otto	Medicine	1922	1884–1951
Michelson, Albert	Physics	1907	1853–1931

Last Name, First Name	Nobel Prize	Year of Award	Born–Died
Milstein, Cesar	Medicine	1984	1927–2002
Moissan, Henri (m)	Chemistry	1906	1852–1907
Mottelson, Benjamin	Physics	1975	1926–2013
Muller, Hermann (m)	Medicine	1946	1890–1967
Müller, Karl (m)	Physics	1987	1927
Nathans, Daniel	Medicine	1978	1928–1999
Nirenberg, Marshall	Medicine	1968	1927–2010
Olah, George	Chemistry	1994	1927–2017
Osheroff, Douglas (f)	Physics	1996	1945
Pauli, Wolfgang (3)	Physics	1945	1900–1958
Penzias, Arno	Physics	1978	1933
Perl, Martin	Physics	1995	1927–2014
Perlmutter, Saul	Physics	2011	1959
Perutz, Max	Chemistry	1962	1914–2002
Polanyi, John (f)	Chemistry	1986	1929–1964
Politzer, David	Physics	2004	1949
Prigogine, Ilya	Chemistry	1977	1917–2003
Prusiner, Stanley	Medicine	1997	1942
Rabi, Isidor	Physics	1944	1898–1988
Reichstein, Tadeus	Medicine	1950	1897–1996
Reines, Frederick	Physics	1995	1918–1998
Richter, Burton	Physics	1976	1931–2018
Riess, Adam	Physics	2011	1969
Rodbell, Martin	Medicine	1994	1925–1998
Rosbash, Michael	Medicine	2017	1944
Rose, Irwin	Chemistry	2004	1926–2015

Last Name, First Name	Nobel Prize	Year of Award	Born–Died
Rothman, James	Medicine	2013	1950
Schawlow, Arthur (f)	Physics	1981	1921–1999
Schekman, Randy	Medicine	2013	1948
Schwartz, Melvin	Physics	1988	1932–2006
Schwinger, Julian	Physics	1965	1918–1994
Segrè, Emilio	Physics	1959	1905–1989
Shechtman, Daniel	Chemistry	2011	1941
Stein, William	Chemistry	1972	1911–1980
Steinberger, Jack	Physics	1988	1921
Steinman, Ralph	Medicine	2011	1943–2011
Stern, Otto	Physics	1943	1888–1969
Temin, Howard	Medicine	1975	1934–1994
Vane, Sir John (f)	Medicine	1982	1927–2004
Varmus, Harold	Medicine	1989	1939
Waksman, Selman	Medicine	1952	1888–1973
Wald, George	Medicine	1967	1906–1997
Wallach, Otto (f)	Chemistry	1910	1847–1931
Warburg, Otto (f)	Medicine	1931	1883–1970
Warshel, Arieh	Chemistry	2013	1940
Weinberg, Steven	Physics	1979	1933
Weiss, Rainer (3)	Physics	2017	1932
Wigner, Eugene	Physics	1963	1902–1995
Willstatter, Richard	Chemistry	1915	1872–1942
Yalow, Rosalyn	Medicine	1977	1921–2011
Yonath, Ada	Chemistry	2009	1939

EXHIBIT II
NOBEL SCIENCE PRIZEWINNERS–
JEWISH PARTICIPATION

1901–2018	Medicine	Physics	Chemistry	Total
Total World Awards	216	210	181	607
Total Jewish Awards	57	56	35	148
% of World Awards	26%	27%	19%	24%
Total U.S. Awards	104	96	75	275
% of World Awards	48%	46%	41%	45%
Jewish American Awards*	43	38	20	101
% of U.S. Awards	41%	40%	27%	37%

*65% U.S.-born / 35% foreign-born U.S. citizens

II. The Rarified World of the Nobel Prize

Dr. Andrew Schally (Medicine, 1976) receives the Nobel Prize from King Carl XVI Gustaf of Sweden.

There is no more meaningful way to measure achievement in science than the Nobel Prize. First awarded in 1901 under the terms of the will of the Swedish industrialist Alfred Nobel (the inventor of dynamite), the Nobel Prize is the most respected and sought-after honor in the world of intellectual achievement. This is especially true of the three Nobel science prizes which are awarded in the fields of medicine, physics, and chemistry. The science prizes gained pre-eminence because of their rigorous and largely impartial selection process. With its unique prestige, the Nobel Prize brings honor not only to the recipients, but also to the nations of their birth (and, when applicable, their adopted countries), as well as the universities and institutions where they studied, conducted research, taught, and worked.

The Nobel prizes for science are awarded for the most important discovery, invention, or improvement in each field. The Royal Swedish Academy of Sciences awards the prizes in physics and chemistry, while the Karolinska (Caroline) Medical Institute, also in Stockholm, awards the prizes for medicine. In each field, the Academy or Institute appoints a committee who thoroughly investigate and recommend candidates. Each committee solicits confidential nominations from hundreds of knowledgeable scientists, university professors and members of scientific institutions, as well as from previous science honorands. The committees consult outside experts to investigate the originality and significance of each nominee's contribution to assure that the selections go to the most meritorious scientists.

Utmost confidentiality prevails throughout the selection process until the awards are announced. Candidates can be nominated numerous times in different years. Sigmund Freud, the psychiatry pioneer, was nominated thirty-two times for a Nobel in medicine, but never received the award as his findings were considered of unproven scientific value. The names of the nominators and nominees cannot be divulged for 50 years.

In addition to the great distinction that the Nobel Prize confers on its recipients, the monetary award that accompanies the award is not insignificant. The total amount has varied greatly depending on the performance of the Nobel Fund's investments. In 2018, each of the six prizes' monetary award was $1.1 million, down from $1.4 million in 2009, reflecting the foundation's investment results. In practice the amount each laureate receives frequently is considerably less, as laureates often share the prize money with one and sometimes two colleagues. Alfred Nobel originally intended to underwrite top scientists' research by providing for their support corresponding to twenty years of salary for a university professor.

The laureates also receive an elaborate personalized diploma and a gold medal, which are presented by the King of Sweden. Resplendent ceremonies in Stockholm celebrate the event which lasts a week and culminates with a sumptuous banquet. The intrinsic value of the 175 grams of the gold in the medal is currently worth in excess of $10,000, but varies with the price of gold. The family of Leon Lederman* sold his Nobel gold medal for $765,000 to cover his medical expenses for dementia. The highest recorded sale belonged to James Watson, the discoverer of the double helix structure of DNA, whose 1962 gold medal was auctioned at Christie's in 2014 for a whopping $4.76 million.[5]

The announcement that they have won a Nobel Prize takes many honorands by surprise. Often the recipients at first think the call is a prank. Some have received the news under unusual circumstances. Robert Barany* (Medicine 1914) was a prisoner of war in Turkestan during World War I. Even the intervention of Swedish royalty could not get him released to receive the award. Jerome Karle[C] first heard that he had won the prize while on a transatlantic flight. The captain of the plane announced the news to the passengers: "We are honored to have flying with us today America's newest Nobel Prize winner and he doesn't even know it. In fact, the award is so recent that Dr. Jerome Karle located in seat 29C left Munich this morning before he could be notified."[6] Irving Wallace's 1962 novel *The Prize*, which was later made into

5 *New York Times*, December 5, 2014

6 Howes, Laura. "Chemistry Laureate Jerome Karle Dies." *Chemistry World,* 21 June 2013

a movie starring Paul Newman, includes fictionalized accounts of winners' reactions on hearing the news.

According to Alfred Nobel's will, the science prizes are to be given for discoveries, inventions, or improvements made in the previous year, not for lifetime achievement. In practice this has not been the case, as it takes years, even decades, to corroborate the viability or effectiveness of a scientific discovery or improvement. Although Sir Alexander Fleming and his collaborator Sir Ernst Chain[M] discovered penicillin in 1928, they did not receive the Nobel Prize in medicine for their finding until 1945, after World War II proved its effectiveness.

More recent examples: John Gurdon received the 2012 prize for medicine for research work done in 1962 using frogs to study stem cells. At the time scientists believed that the discovery had no therapeutic applications. Fifty years later further research confirmed that scientists can reprogram ordinary human stem cells into many different body cells. The existence of the Higgs Boson (also known as the "God particle") was theorized in the 1960s. However, it was not until 2013, when a sufficiently powerful particle accelerator—the Hadron Collider at CERN (European Organization for Nuclear Research)—confirmed their findings, that Peter Higgs and Francois Englert[P] were awarded the Nobel Prize in physics.

Sometimes a Nobel award is not for an honoree's most recognized achievement. Such was the case with Albert Einstein.* He was awarded the 1921 prize in physics for his discovery of the photo-electric effect, rather than for his more abstract theory of relativity, whose revolutionary impact was not fully recognized at the time. Einstein's genius lives on: The 2017 prize in Physics was awarded to Barry Barish[P], Rainer Weiss[P], and Kip Thorne who were able to confirm his theory about gravitational waves which he had predicted a hundred years earlier.

The Nobel Prize rules stipulate that no more than three persons can share a prize. In modern scientific research, in which several scientists may be working simultaneously on the same project, sharing the prize among two and even three honorands has become increasingly common. This raises the question: Does a single prizewinner have more merit than those who were awarded the prize jointly? Perhaps a single prizewinner is more deserving in some cases, but not in all. In practice the Nobel Foundation makes no distinction except for the division of the prize's monetary reward. Likewise all prizewinners receive equal standing herein whether their prize was shared or received solo.

Peter Higgs and Francois Englert (left) at CERN on 4 July 2012.

Sometimes scientists who win Nobel Prizes jointly work together cooperatively in the same research facility or in distant labs. They may also work independently on the same project without communicating with each other. Such was the case of Peter Higgs and Francois Englert[P] (Physics 2013), who worked independently on the Higgs Boson "God" particle and did not meet until they received the Nobel Prize in Stockholm.

On the other hand Andrew Schally and Roger Guillemin (both Medicine 1977) were fiercely competitive. Their struggle is chronicled in the 1981 book by Nicholas Ware, *The Nobel Duel, Two Scientists' 21 Year Race to Win the World's Most Coveted Prize.*

The average age of receiving a Nobel Prize in the three categories of science ranges between 55 and 58 years old. The youngest recipient is 25-year-old Sir Walter Bragg (Physics 1915). The oldest person is Arthur Ashkin,* who was 96 years old when he was awarded the Nobel Prize in physics in 2018. The Nobel Prize honorand who lived the longest is Rita Levi-Montalcini* (Medicine 1986), who died at the age of 103 in 2013.

One of the notable rules governing the Nobel prizes is that they may not be awarded posthumously. However, ailing and near death, Ralph Steinman[M] (Medicine 2001), who believed that he was going to receive the award, is reported to have clung to life as long as possible. He died three days before the announcement that he had won the prize, but his family did not reveal his death until after the award was announced. Nevertheless, the Nobel committee members decided not to rescind the award since they were not aware of his demise.

In retrospect it is not surprising that some honorands may not have been the most deserving. The Nobel science awards have not been without possible omissions of worthy candidates. Among Jewish scientists passed over are Carl Djerassi and Gregory Pincus, creators of the birth control pill, Theodore Maiman, who invented the laser, and Paul Zoll, a pioneer developer of the cardiac pacemaker and defibrillator.

Gregory Pincus, co-creator of the birth control pill.

Best known, however, is Jonas Salk, usually credited with the discovery of the poliovirus vaccine. Although he was nominated several times, the committee deemed that the Nobel Prize for the basic discovery had already been awarded to John Enders (Medicine 1954), and his collaborators, Thomas Weller and Frederick Robbins, for successfully growing the poliomyelitis virus in cultures of human tissue. Dr. Sven Gard, Professor of Virology at the Karolinska Institute, provided what perhaps is a disappointing explanation. He convinced the Nobel committee that, "Salk has not, in the development of his methods, introduced anything that is principally new, but only exploited discoveries made by others."[7]

Overall, there has been remarkably little controversy about the merit and credibility of the awards for scientific discoveries. One of the most notorious cases in retrospect was awarding Antonio Egas Moniz the 1949 prize in medicine for his work on the therapeutic value of lobotomy (the removal of the front lobe of the brain), which has long since been discredited.

---

7 Racaniello, Vincent. "Polio and Nobel Prizes." 7 Sept. 2007

Jonas Salk at the University of Pittsburg, where
he developed the first polio vaccine.

A controversial occurrence involved David Baltimore[M] (Medicine 1975) and his assistant Thereza Imanishi-Kari. She was accused of presenting fraudulent results of a scientific investigation. Baltimore's reputation was tarnished by vigorously defending her. After many years of investigations that went all the way to U.S. Congressional hearings, they were exonerated. At the time, however, Baltimore had to resign the presidency of Rockefeller University, but later was appointed President of the California Institute of Technology. Less involved was the case of Selman Waksman* (Medicine 1952) who discovered streptomycin, the first antibiotic drug effective against tuberculosis. A Rutgers University lab assistant claimed that he unfairly was left out of Waksman's award. The Nobel Committee looked into the allegations and upheld Waksman's sole award.

For a hundred and eighteen years, knowledgeable scientists worldwide have generally held the selection of Nobel science prizewinners in the highest esteem, thereby maintaining the continued prestige of the awards. The same cannot be said about the Nobel prizes for literature and peace, which differ markedly from those awarded for the sciences. Unlike the science awards, these awards cannot be subject to objective evaluation. The wisdom of these selections has often been questioned. Jewish prizewinners are also disproportionately represented in the other Nobel prize awards—literature, peace, and economics.

Appreciation of works of literature by its very nature lends itself to being highly subjective. Judging and evaluating works written in different languages makes comparisons even more difficult. There are an impressive fourteen Jewish literature laureates. They include such authors as Boris Pasternak, Saul Bellow, Isaac Bashevis Singer, Nadine Gordimer, playwright Harold Pinter, and in 2018, musician Bob Dylan "for having created new poetic expressions within the great American song tradition." Others such as Paul Heyse, Henri Bergson, Yosef Agnon, Nelly Sachs, Elias Canetti, Joseph Brodsky, Imre Kertesz, and Elfriede Jelinek may be less known or not known at all by the general public.

The Peace Prize, awarded by the Norwegian Nobel Committee in Oslo, is the most controversial of all the Nobel Prize awards and the only one not awarded by Swedish institutions. Unlike all the other Nobel awards' selection processes, the Peace Prize is determined by a committee of five Norwegian parliamentarians who choose the nominees as well as the winners. Their selections have often been criticized as questionable as in the case of Yasser Arafat, or inspired by political events or personalities of the moment, such as President Barack Obama, who received the prize only nine months into his presidency (he donated the award money of 1.1 million dollars to charities). In 1991 there was a movement to revoke the award of Aung San Suu Kyi when, as Prime Minister of Myanmar, she took no action to stop the persecution of the Rohingya, Myanmar's Muslim minority. The Nobel organization, however, stated that it does not revoke prizes.

There are nine Jewish Peace Prize laureates including such prominent figures as Menachem Begin, Henry Kissinger, Elie Wiesel, Yitzhak Rabin, and Shimon Peres, as well as such obscure persons as Tobias Asser, Alfred Fried, Rene Cassin, and Joseph Rotblat.

The Nobel Prize for economics is of relatively recent creation, and was not one of the original awards that Alfred Nobel designated in his will. Created to mark the 300th anniversary of the Bank of Sweden, the economics prize has been accepted as a worthy distinction by the Royal Swedish Academy of Sciences and abides by the same rules and principles that guide the original Nobel Prizes. It has been awarded only since 1969 and is officially known as The Alfred Nobel Memorial Prize for Economic Sciences.

Economics, "the dismal science" of Adam Smith, is anything but an exact science since the findings are not subject to proof. They are often questionable and colored by the honorees' political orientation. Laureates include such widely disparate economists as Milton Friedman and Paul Krugman, whose views represent opposite ends of the economic political spectrum. The percentage of Jews who have received the Nobel Prize in economics exceeds even the number in the science categories attesting once again to their vast overachievement. In the 50 years since the economics prize was first awarded, there have been 81 Nobel economists; 32 or 40% are of Jewish origin. Americans account for an overwhelming 73% off all honorands in this category, with Jewish Americans accounting for more than half (54%) of the U.S. awards.

EXHIBIT III
JEWISH NOBEL PRIZEWINNERS
REASON FOR AWARD BY CATEGORY

MEDICINE

Name	Year of Award	Reasons for Award (Information from Nobel Prize citations)
Michael Rosbash	2017	"For discoveries of molecular mechanisms controlling the circadian rhythm" (shared)
James Rothman Randy Schekman	2013	"For their discoveries of machinery regulating vesicle traffic, a major transport system in our cells" (shared)
Ralph Steinman Bruce Beutler	2011	S: "For his discovery of the dendritic cell and its role in adaptive immunity" (shared) B: "For discoveries concerning the activation of innate immunity" (shared)
Andrew Fire	2006	"For discovery of RNA interference—gene silencing by double-stranded RNA" (shared)
Richard Axel	2004	"For discoveries of odorant receptors and the organization of the olfactory system" (shared)
Sydney Brenner H. Robert Horvitz	2002	"For their discoveries concerning genetic regulation of organ development and programmed cell death" (shared)
Paul Greengard Eric Kandel	2000	"For their discoveries concerning signal transduction in the nervous system" (shared)
Robert Furchgott	1998	"For discoveries concerning nitric oxide as a signaling molecule in the cardiovascular system" (shared)
Stanley Prusiner	1997	"For his discovery of Prions—a new biological principle of infection."

Name	Year of Award	Reasons for Award (Information from Nobel Prize citations)
Alfred Gilman Martin Rodbell	1994	"For their discovery of G-proteins and the role of these proteins in signal transduction in cells." (shared)
Edmond Fischer	1992	"For discoveries concerning reversible protein phosphorylation as a biological regulatory mechanism" (shared)
Harold Varmus	1989	"For discovery of the cellular origin of retroviral oncogenes" (shared)
Gertrude Elion	1988	"For discoveries of important principles for drug treatment" (shared)
Stanley Cohen Rita Levi-Montalcini	1986	"For their discoveries of growth factors" (shared)
Michael Brown Joseph Goldstein	1985	"For their discoveries concerning the regulation of cholesterol metabolism" (shared)
Cesar Milstein	1984	"For theories concerning the specificity in development and control of the immune system and the discovery of the principle for production of monoclonal antibodies" (shared)
John Vane	1982	"For discoveries concerning prostaglandins and related biologically active substances" (shared)
Baruj Benacerraf	1980	"For discoveries concerning genetically determined structures on the cell surface that regulate immunological reactions" (shared)
Daniel Nathans	1978	"For the discovery of restriction enzymes and their application to problems of molecular genetics" (shared)
Rosalyn Yalow	1977	"For the development of radioimmunoassays of peptide hormones" (shared)
Baruch Blumberg	1976	"For discoveries concerning new mechanisms for the origin and dissemination of infectious diseases" (shared)

Name	Year of Award	Reasons for Award (Information from Nobel Prize citations)
David Baltimore Howard Temin	1975	"For discoveries concerning the interaction between tumor viruses and the genetic material of the cell" (shared)
Gerald Edelman	1972	"For discoveries concerning the chemical structure of antibodies" (shared)
Julius Axelrod Bernard Katz, Sir	1970	"For their discoveries concerning the humoral transmittors in the nerve terminals and the mechanism for their storage, release and inactivation" (shared)
Salvador Luria	1969	"For discoveries concerning the replication mechanism and the genetic structure of viruses" (shared)
Marshall Nirenberg	1968	"For interpretation of the genetic code and its function in protein synthesis" (shared)
George Wald	1967	"For discoveries concerning the primary physiological and chemical visual processes in the eye" (shared)
Francois Jacob Andre Lwoff	1965	"For discoveries concerning genetic control of enzyme and virus synthesis" (shared)
Konrad Bloch	1964	"For discoveries concerning the mechanism and regulation of the cholesterol and fatty acid metabolism" (shared)
Arthur Kornberg	1959	"For discovery of the mechanisms in the biological synthesis of ribonucleic acid and deoxyribonucleic acid" (shared)
Joshua Lederberg	1958	"For his discoveries [on] genetic recombination and the organization of the genetic material of bacteria" (shared)
Hans Krebs, Sir Fritz Lipmann	1953	Krebs: "For his discovery of the citric acid cycle" Lipmann: "For his discovery of co-enzyme A and its importance for intermediary metabolism"

Name	Year of Award	Reasons for Award (Information from Nobel Prize citations)
Selman Waksman	1952	"For his discovery of streptomycin, the first antibiotic effective against tuberculosis"
Tadeus Reichstein	1950	"For discoveries relating to the hormones of the adrenal cortex, their structure and biological effects" (shared)
Gerty Radnitz Cori	1947	"For discovery of the course of the catalytic conversion of glycogen" (shared)
Hermann Muller	1946	"For the discovery of the production of mutations by means of X-ray irradiation"
Ernst Chain, Sir	1945	"For the discovery of penicillin and its curative effect in various infectious diseases" (shared)
Joseph Erlanger Herbert Gasser	1944	"For their discoveries relating to the highly differentiated functions of single nerve fibers"
Otto Loewi	1936	"For discoveries relating to chemical transmission of nerve impulses" (shared)
Otto Warburg	1931	"For his discovery of the nature and mode of action of the respiratory enzyme"
Karl Landsteiner	1930	"For his discovery of human blood groups"
Otto Meyerhof	1922	"For his discovery of the fixed relationship between the consumption of oxygen and the metabolism of lactic acid in the muscle" (shared)
Robert Barany	1914	"For his work on the physiology and pathology of the vestibular apparatus"
Paul Ehrlich Ilya Metchnikoff	1908	"In recognition of their work on immunity" (shared)

PHYSICS

Name	Year of Award	Reasons for Award (Information from Nobel Prize citations)
Arthur Ashkin	2018	"For the optical tweezers and their application to biological systems."
Barry Barish Rainer Weiss	2017	"For decisive contributions to the LIGO detector and the observation of gravitational waves" (shared)
J. Michael Kosterlitz	2016	"For theoretical discoveries of topological phase transitions and topological phases of matter" (shared)
Francois Englert	2013	"For the theoretical discovery of a mechanism that contributes to our understanding of the origin of mass subatomic particles" (shared)
Serge Haroche	2012	"For ground-breaking experimental methods that enable measuring and manipulation of individual quantum systems" (shared)
Saul Perlmutter Adam Riess	2011	"For the discovery of the accelerating expansion of the Universe through observations of distant supernovae" (shared)
Roy Glauber	2005	"For his contribution to the quantum theory of optical coherence" (shared)
David Gross David Politzer	2004	"For the discovery of asymptotic freedom in the theory of the strong interaction" (shared)
Alexei Abrikosov Vitaly Ginzburg	2003	"For pioneering contributions to the theory of superconductors and superfluids" (shared)
Zhores Alferov	2000	"For basic work on information and communication technology" (shared)
Claude Cohen-Tannoudji	1997	"For development of methods to cool and trap atoms with laser light" (shared)
David Lee Douglas Osheroff	1996	"For their discovery of superfluidity in helium-3" (shared)

Name	Year of Award	Reasons for Award (Information from Nobel Prize citations)
Martin Perl Frederick Reines	1995	"For pioneering experimental contributions to lepton physics" P: "For the discovery of the tau lepton" R: "For the detection of the neutrino" (shared)
Georges Charpak	1992	"For his invention and development of particle detectors, in particular the multiwire proportional chamber"
Jerome Friedman	1990	"For pioneering investigations concerning deep inelastic scattering of electrons on protons and bound neutrons…of essential importance for the development of the quark model in particle physics" (shared)
Leon Lederman Melvin Schwartz Jack Steinberger	1988	"For the neutrino beam method and the demonstration of the doublet structure of the leptons through the discovery of the muon neutrino" (shared)
Karl Alexander Müller	1987	"For an important breakthrough in the discovery of super-conductivity in ceramic materials" (shared)
Arthur Schawlow	1981	"For [his] contribution to the development of laser spectroscopy" (shared)
Sheldon Glashow Steven Weinberg	1979	"For their contributions to the theory of the unified weak and electromagnetic interaction between elementary particles" (shared)
Pyotr Kapitsa Arno Penzias	1978	K: "For his basic inventions and discoveries in the area of low temperature physics" (shared) P: "For discovery of cosmic microwave background radiation" (shared)
Burton Richter	1976	"For pioneering work in the discovery of a heavy elementary particle of a new kind" (shared)
Benjamin Mottelson	1975	"For the discovery of the connection between collective motion and particle motion in atomic nuclei and the development of the theory of the structure of the atomic nucleus based on this connection" (shared)

Name	Year of Award	Reasons for Award (Information from Nobel Prize citations)
Brian Josephson	1973	"For his theoretical predictions of the properties of a supercurrent through a tunnel barrier, in particular, known as the Josephson effects" (shared)
Leon Cooper	1972	"For [the] jointly developed theory of superconductivity, usually called the BCS-theory" (shared)
Dennis Gabor	1971	"For his invention and development of the holographic method"
Murray Gell-Mann	1969	"For his contributions and discoveries concerning the classification of elementary particles and their interactions"
Hans Bethe	1967	"For his contributions to the theory of nuclear reactions, especially his discoveries concerning the energy production in stars"
Richard Feynman Julian Schwinger	1965	"For their fundamental work in quantum electro-dynamics, with deep-ploughing consequences for the physics of elementary particles" (shared)
Eugene Wigner	1963	"For his contributions to the theory of the atomic nucleus and the elementary particles, particularly through the discovery and application of fundamental symmetry principles" (shared)
Lev Landau	1962	"For his pioneering theories for condensed matter, especially liquid helium"
Robert Hofstadter	1961	"For his pioneering studies of electron scattering in atomic nuclei and for...discoveries concerning the structure of the nucleons" (shared)
Donald Glaser	1960	"For the invention of the bubble chamber"
Emilio Segrè	1959	"For discovery of the antiproton" (shared)
Ilya Frank	1958	"For the discovery and the interpretation of the Cherenkov effect" in electromagnetic radiation (shared)

Name	Year of Award	Reasons for Award (Information from Nobel Prize citations)
Max Born	1954	"For his fundamental research in quantum mechanics, especially for his statistical interpretation of the wavefunction" (shared)
Felix Bloch	1952	"For…development of new methods for nuclear magnetic precision measurements" (shared)
Wolfgang Pauli	1945	"For the discovery of the Exclusion Principle, also called the Pauli Principle" (quantum mechanics)
Isidor Rabi	1944	"For his resonance method for recording the magnetic properties of atomic nuclei"
Otto Stern	1943	"For his contribution to the development of the molecular ray method and his discovery of the magnetic moment of the proton"
James Franck Gustav Hertz	1925	"For their discovery of the laws governing the impact of an electron upon an atom" (shared)
Niels Bohr	1922	"For his services in the investigation of the structure of atoms and of the radiation emanating from them"
Albert Einstein	1921	"For his services to theoretical physics, and especially for his discovery of the law of the photoelectric effect"
Gabriel Lippmann	1908	"For his method of reproducing colors photographically based on the phenomenon of interference"
Albert Michelson	1907	"For his optical precision instruments and the spectroscopic and meteorological investigations carried out with their aid"

CHEMISTRY

Name	Year of Award	Reasons for Award (Information from Nobel Prize citations)
Martin Karplus Michael Levitt Arieh Warshel	2013	"For the development of multiscale models for complex chemical systems" (shared)
Robert Lefkowitz	2012	"For studies of G-protein-coupled receptors" (shared)
Daniel Shechtman	2011	"For the discovery of quasicrystals"
Ada Yonath	2009	"For studies on the structure and function of the ribosome" (shared)
Martin Chalfie	2008	"For the discovery and development of the green fluorescent protein, GFP" (shared)
Roger Kornberg	2006	"For his studies of the molecular basis of eukaryotic transcription"
Aaron Ciechanover Avram Hersko Irwin Rose	2004	"For the discovery of ubiquitin-mediated protein degradation" (shared)
Alan Heeger	2000	"For the discovery and development of conductive polymers" (shared)
Walter Kohn	1998	"For his development of the density-functional theory" (shared)
Harold Kroto, Sir	1996	"For discovery of fullerenes" (shared)
George Olah	1994	"For his contribution to carbocation chemistry"
Rudolph Marcus	1992	"For his contribution to the theory of electron transfer reactions in chemical systems"
Sidney Altman	1989	"For discovery of catalytic properties of RNA" (shared)
John Polanyi	1986	"For contributions concerning the dynamics of chemical elementary processes" (shared)

Name	Year of Award	Reasons for Award (Information from Nobel Prize citations)
Herbert Hauptman Jerome Karle	1985	"For their outstanding achievements in the development of direct methods for the determination of crystal structures (shared)
Aaron Klug, Sir	1982	"For his development of crystallographic electron microscopy and his structural elucidation of biologically important nucleic acid-protein complexes"
Roald Hoffmann	1981	"For theories, developed independently, [on] the course of chemical reactions" (shared)
Walter Gilbert Paul Berg	1980	G: "For contributions concerning the determination of base sequences in nucleic acids" (shared) B: "For his fundamental studies of the biochemistry of nucleic acids, with particular regard to recombinant DNA"
Herbert Brown	1979	"For development of the use of boron- and phosphorus-containing compounds into important reagents in organic synthesis" (shared)
Ilya Prigogine	1977	"For contributions to nonequilibrium thermodynamics, particularly the theory of dissipative structures"
William Stein	1972	"For contributions to the understanding of the connection between chemical structure and catalytic activity of the active center of the ribonuclease molecule" (shared)
Max Perutz	1962	"For studies of the structures of globular proteins" (shared)
Melvin Calvin	1961	"For research on the carbon dioxide assimilation in plants"
George de Hevesy	1943	"For his work on the use of isotopes as tracers in the study of chemical processes"
Fritz Haber	1918	"For the synthesis of ammonia from its elements"

Name	Year of Award	Reasons for Award (Information from Nobel Prize citations)
Richard Willstatter	1915	"For his research on plant pigments, especially chlorophyll"
Otto Wallach	1910	"In recognition of his services to organic chemistry and the chemical industry by his pioneer work in the field of alicyclic compounds"
Henri Moissan	1906	"In recognition of the great services rendered by him in his investigation and isolation of the element fluorine, and for the adoption in the service of science of the electric furnace named after him"
Adolph von Baeyer	1905	"In recognition of his services in the advancement of organic chemistry and the chemical industry, through his work on organic dyes and hydroaromatic compounds."

III. Who's Counted?

Who is Jewish? I am not concerned with rabbinical laws that Judaism is transmitted through the mother or by Orthodox conversion, nor the State of Israel's immigration policy determining who is eligible for the law of return. For purposes of this work, anyone whose parents were Jewish is considered to be a Jew, no matter what they consider themselves. Jews who have converted, those who are indifferent to Judaism, agnostics and atheists are counted as long as at least one parent is Jewish. Who is counted is based on ethnic origin rather than religious belief or affiliation.

Those Nobelists who have only one Jewish parent (either one) are counted and are included among the 148 Jewish Nobel prizewinners. Clearly a person is the result of both parents and represents a comingling of their genetic make-up though the extent of influence of each is unknown. I am reminded of a personal anecdote. With a Jewish father and a Protestant mother, my six-year-old daughter, when told that she was half-Jewish, promptly asked, "Which half?"

As best I can determine, 23 (16%) of the laureates were born to only one Jewish parent. Mothers and fathers account for 10 each, and two have three Jewish grandparents. These half-Jewish prizewinners are noted in Exhibit I, which also indicates which parent is Jewish. Identifying the children of parents in a mixed marriage may not always be evident.

Take the case of Andrew Schally (Medicine 1977). Sometimes the information available about the laureates' Jewish lineage is contradictory or inadequate. There is conflicting information about his ethnic and religious background. One could presume that at least one of his parents was Jewish based on this statement in his autobiography: "I was fortunate to survive the Holocaust while living among the Jewish-Polish community in Roumania. I used

Dr. Andrew Schally and the author, Ronald Gerstl

to speak Polish, Roumanian, Yiddish, Italian, and some German and Russian."[8] It so happens that I had the opportunity to meet with Dr. Schally, as he is the only Nobel prizewinner in science living in Miami, where I reside. He is a remarkable man, who was still working full time at 88 as a Distinguished Medical Scientist with the U.S. Veteran's Administration and as an emeritus faculty member at the University of Miami's Medical School. Dr. Schally

---

8 "Andrew V. Schally—Biographical." *Nobelprize.org.*

appeared to be somewhat uncertain about his family's religious origins. He was baptized Catholic, but believes that there may have been some Jewish background in his family. The family may have distanced themselves from their Jewish roots. With rising antisemitism in pre-World War II Europe, many people sought to conceal their Jewish past. In any case, Schally is not counted among the Jewish Nobel prizewinners in science.

Another case that was difficult to determine was Pyotr Kapitsa,* the 1978 physics laureate. Several sources cite him as having a Jewish mother. He was an active participant in the Jewish anti-fascist committee and, in 1941, a speaker at the rally of the representatives of the Jewish people in Moscow. Still, there is some question whether he had any Jewish parentage. Until there is more evidence to the contrary, we have included him as half Jewish.

Wolfgang Pauli's* (Physics 1945) Jewish father converted to Catholicism upon marriage to a Catholic woman whose father was Jewish. Although brought up in his mother's faith, he considered himself agnostic. Three of his four grandparents were Jewish. Paul Greengard* (Medicine 2000) had a Jewish mother who died giving birth to him. His father then married an Episcopalian woman who brought him up in her religion. Both Nobelists are counted.

It was not uncommon for Jews to convert to Christianity in pre-WWII Germany and the former Austro-Hungarian Empire in order to assimilate and progress in the broader society in which they lived. The parents of Max Perutz[C] (Chemistry 1962) had him baptized at birth to open opportunities for him. As it turned out, Perutz later rejected Catholicism and became an atheist. Conversion was also often convenient in order to further one's education or to advance one's career (like composers Mendelssohn and Mahler). In the same vein, although both parents of Fritz Haber*

(Chemistry 1918) were Jewish, he converted to Lutheranism as a young man. Both Perutz and Haber are counted.

Gerty Theresa Radnitz Cori and her husband Carl Cori
were jointly awarded the Nobel Prize in medicine in 1947.

Sometimes it was marriage that necessitated conversion to Christianity. Such was the case for Gerty Radnitz Cori* (Medicine 1947) whose in-laws insisted that she convert to Catholicism in order to marry their son, Carl Cori (Medicine 1947). Max Born* (Physics 1954) converted to Lutheranism upon marriage to please his Lutheran wife. Both are counted. Then there is the extreme case of Karl Landsteiner* (Medicine 1930), who was born to Jewish parents and converted to Catholicism. Such was his renunciation of his Jewish origins that he brought a lawsuit against the publishers of a Jewish *Who's Who* for including him. He is counted. (Sorry, Mr. Landsteiner.)

On the other hand, Christian Anfinsen (Chemistry 1972) presents a uniquely reverse case. Of Norwegian Lutheran stock, he converted to Judaism, becoming Orthodox no less. In 1978, he married Libby Esther Shulman Ely, presumably Jewish, who may have played a role in his conversion. In 1985, he wrote in his biography, "Although my feelings about religion still very strongly reflect a fifty-year period of orthodox agnosticism, I must say that I do find the history, practice, and intensity of Judaism an extremely interesting philosophic package."[9] He is not counted.

Christian Anfinsen

In closing: It is possible that I may have misclassified some Nobel Prize laureates as Jewish or half-Jewish who are not. I hope I will not be sued! If there is a third edition, I will rectify the data accordingly.

---

9 *The Christian B. Anfinsen Papers. Nobelprize.org.* National Library of Medicine Profiles in Science

IV. Laureates' National
and Ethnic Backgrounds

"If I am correct the Germans will call me a German,
the Swiss will call me a Swiss citizen, and the French will
call me a great scientist. If relativity is proved wrong,
the French will call me a Swiss, the Swiss will call me
a German, and the Germans will call me a Jew."

—ALBERT EINSTEIN on presenting a paper on the then
questionable theory of relativity in 1921 at the Sorbonne in Paris.
(He became a Swiss citizen while living in Switzerland.)

Like universities and other entities, nations like to bask in the glory of Nobel laureates they can claim as their own, but that regard is not always reciprocated. When hailed in Austria for his Nobel Prize in Medicine in 2000, Vienna-born Eric Kandel,* who had fled the country when he was nine years old, stated emphatically: "Certainly not an Austrian Nobel, it was a Jewish American Nobel."[10]

In his will Alfred Nobel stated that nationality should not be a factor in awarding prizes. Nevertheless there is likely to be some natural favoritism for Scandinavians, especially in the subjective

---

10 *Science Magazine*. 16 June, 2008

category of literature. Overall, the United States has clearly out-distanced all other nations in the total number of Nobel science prizewinners. Britain and Germany are in a distant second place, with France ranking fourth. Among these four leading nations on a per capita basis Britain ranked first by a wide margin, followed by Germany, the United States, and France. Germany and France were strongest in the earlier years of the twentieth century. On a per capita basis, the United States peaked in the 1970s, partly due to the coming of age of refugee scientists uprooted by Nazism. More recently Britain has out-paced the United States.

Eric Kandel, Medicine
Nobelist, 2000

When all countries are ranked on a per capita basis, Switzerland ranks first followed by Austria, Sweden, Denmark, Norway, Great Britain, Hungary, the Netherlands, Germany, and the United States in tenth place.[11] Israel, a nation only since 1948, occupies the eleventh place. A couple of caveats: the list compilation also includes Nobel Memorial Prize in Economic Sciences as well as the prizes for medicine, physics and chemistry; however, that should not make a substantial difference. The countries' rankings may not be in the same order as on the list, but there is little doubt that these nations are among the highest ranking in science honorands. The bottom of the listing includes some nations with huge populations, such as China, India, and Pakistan. Some other very populous nations, such as Indonesia and Nigeria, have not received a Nobel science prize.

---

11 Compiled by BBC News, 2017.

Among Jewish American laureates, about two-thirds were born in the United States, while one-third were born abroad and became U.S. citizens. The first U.S. citizen to win any Nobel science prize, not just Jewish American laureates, was Prussian-born, U.S. Naval Academy graduate Albert Michelson* in 1907.

Albert Michelson, the first American Nobel science prizewinner

While it is common for foreign-born scientists to acquire U.S. citizenship, Benjamin Mottelson[P] (Physics 1975) is the unique exception of an American settling abroad and adopting another nationality. The Chicago-born laureate acquired Danish national-ity when he moved to Denmark to work with Niels Bohr* (Physics 1922). He is counted for both nations, as are all laureates herein who acquired a second nationality.

Overall Germany ranks second as the birthplace of Jewish science prizewinners with 22 laureates, followed by the former Austro-Hungarian Empire with 13 (all but one born in either Vienna or Budapest). All of them were born before World War II. Not surprisingly, there has not been a Jewish science laureate born in Germany since 1933, the year Hitler came to power. Russia ranks fourth with nine Jewish science laureates born in Russia (the U.S.S.R. or Russian Empire), demonstrating particular strength in physics. There is no correlation between the Jewish population of a country of birth and its number of Jewish Nobel science prize recipients. Pre-Nazi Germany had a Jewish population of 645,000 and accounted for 22 Jewish Nobel science prizewinners. Poland, which had more than 3,000,000 Jews, accounted for only three or four. Italy, with a very small Jewish community, produced three laureates.

Prior to World War II the Jewish laureates' geographical origins were largely concentrated in German-influenced central Europe. More recently, however, U.S.-born Jewish Americans laureates are more often children of Polish and Russian immigrants. The two major geographical groupings have discernible socioeconomic and cultural differences. Jewish Nobel science prizewinners from Central Europe (Germany and the Austro-Hungarian Empire) and Western Europe (principally England and France) usually came from middle to upper class backgrounds. Their parents by and large were educated professionals who lived in urbanized areas where there were better educational facilities, and where they were exposed to diverse people.

By way of contrast, those living in Eastern Europe in what came to be known as the "Pale of Settlements" usually had different socioeconomic backgrounds. Jews were allowed to live in these territories, then a part of the Russian Empire extending from what is now Lithuania through Poland, Belarus, to the Ukraine. Their rulers viewed Jewish residents as an undesirable minority and they were subject to constant harassment and pillaging and worse, killed in pogroms. As a result, opportunities for education and choices of livelihood were highly limited. Not surprisingly, they were usually poor, had little formal education, were religiously traditional, and tended to favor socialism (think *Fiddler On The Roof*). Even within Russia there was a marked difference between those Jews living in *shtetls* in the Pale and residents of urban centers such as Moscow and St. Petersburg/Leningrad.

The major sub-groups of Jews, the Ashkenazim (derived from Ashkenaz Hebrew for Germany) and the Sephardim (derived from Sepharad, Hebrew for Spain) have distinctive cultures and traditions. Prior to the Holocaust Ashkenazi Jews accounted for more than 90% all Jews. Their number now is estimated at 74%. Historically speaking the Ashkenazi Jews lived largely in Central and Western Europe in the Middle Ages. They were segregated into ghettos, forced to wear distinctive clothes, and limited in the occupations they could practice. By the end of Middle Ages, they were steadily pushed eastward into Poland and Russian territories by persistent persecution engendered by the Catholic Church,

which blamed the Jews for the Black Death plague and other calamities. The Church even propagated "the blood libel," which charged Jews with killing Christian children for their blood to make *matzoh*.

Likewise, the hostility of the Reformation's Martin Luther also contributed to the eastward migration. In his 65,000-word antisemitic diatribe.[12] Luther urged the destruction of Jews' synagogues, schools, and homes, and

Title page of Martin Luther's
On the Jews and Their Lies.

---

12 Luther, Martin. *Von den Jüden und iren Lügen,* Wittenberg, 1543.

confiscation of their property. Those who would not heed the call for expulsion should be slain.

The Sephardic Jews are the descendants of those who lived in the Iberian Peninsula, Spain and Portugal. By the end of the fifteenth century, the Spanish Jews were forced to convert to Catholicism or be expelled from Spain (and, somewhat later, from Portugal). These Sephardic Jews settled largely in Muslim lands in North Africa (Morocco, Algeria, Tunisia, Libya, and Egypt) and the Middle East (Turkey, Syria, Iraq, and Iran), which became part of the Ottoman Empire. Sephardic Jews are a minority within a minority.

The Mizrahi Jews are an even smaller sub-set than the Sephardim. They are the descendants of Jewish communities in the Middle East, central Asia, and the Arabian peninsula who dwelled in such lands as the Levant, Mesopotamia, Persia, and Yemen from biblical times on. The *Mizrahim* (from the Hebrew word for "Eastern") are usually lumped together with the Sephardim since there is a great deal of geographical overlap. The Sephardim, after their expulsion from Iberia, settled in traditionally Mizrahi lands and intermarried with them. The overriding majority of the Mizrahim now live in Israel, having been driven from their homes in the Arab-Muslim world after the creation of the State of Israel. Though the Ashkenazi Jews remain dominant in the country's leadership, the Sephardim and Mizrahim constitute at least half of Israel's population, and are the fastest growing segment.

Even taking into consideration the Sephardim's much smaller numbers, their achievement level is nowhere near that of the Ashkenazim. That said, Sephardic Jews are still vastly over-represented as Nobel science prizewinners in relation to their small number. To have even one Sephardic science laureate would be notable, but there are many more. It does not appear that any of the Nobel prizewinners in science are of Mizrahi origin.

The Sephardim attained high levels of culture and achievement in medieval Spain, superior at the time to their Ashkenazi brethren. Yet, when Europe awoke with the renaissance of learning, the world of Islam where the Sephardim dwelt did not keep pace and lost ground from which it has never recovered. Jews living in Muslim-dominated lands were likewise negatively affected. Scientific activity did not flourish in societies that clung to religious orthodoxy and were not receptive to new ideas and progress. The lack of these educational and cultural values goes a long way in explaining the different level of achievement of Sephardic and Askenazi Jews. The science laureates of Sephardic origin were educated and shaped in advanced countries with highly developed secular educational institutions and outlook.

At least three Jewish science laureates are clearly of Sephardic parentage, and have their origins in the former French North African colonies. Baruj Benacerraf[*] (Medicine 1980) was born in Caracas, Venezuela, to Moroccan/Algerian parents. He was educated in the United States and became a naturalized American. Claude Cohen-Tannoudji[P] (Physics 1997) was born in Constantine, Algeria. At the time of the Inquisition, his family fled Spain for Tangier (Tannoudji in Arabic).

Serge Haroche

He is a French citizen since Algeria was then a French territory, and he was educated in France. Recent laureate, Serge Haroche[P]

(Physics 2012), was born in Morocco, which also was French at the time, and like Cohen-Tannoudji, is also a French citizen educated in France. All three Jewish Italian science laureates—Emilio Segrè* (Physics 1959), Salvador Luria* (Medicine 1969), and Rita Levi-Montalcini* (Medicine 1986)—are also at least partially of Sephardic heritage.

The phenomenon of disproportionate Jewish achievement becomes even more pronounced when one considers that it is highly concentrated among Ashkenazi Jews, who may number only around ten million, which makes their accomplishments even more remarkable.

Europeans and their descendants in the United States, whether Christians or Jews, have dominated the Nobel Prizes in science. In spite of Asia's enormous population, Asian participation has lagged far behind with only 6% of the world's total. Japan is by far the leading Asian contributor to the Nobel roster, with some 60% of the honorands. Japanese science Nobelists have largely been educated and have had their careers in Japan itself. There are only four science prizewinners from the People's Republic of China. Three studied and/or worked in the United States and became naturalized U.S. citizens. The most recent Nobelist, Youyou Tu (Medicine 2013), has remained in China. In addition there are five Nobel science prizewinners of Chinese origin—three U.S. born, one from Hong Kong and one from Taiwan. India accounted for six science laureates.

There have been only three science prizewinners from the Muslim world. The first was Adbus Salam (Physics 1979), a Cambridge University-educated Pakistani, who taught at the University of Cambridge and the Imperial College of London. Egyptian-born Ahmed Zewail (Chemistry 1999), a graduate of the University of

Pennsylvania, is currently a professor at the California Institute of Technology. The most recent Muslim prizewinner, Aziz Sacar (Chemistry 2015), was born in Turkey. He received his Ph.D. from the University of Dallas and has spent most of his career as a professor teaching at the University of North Carolina at Chapel Hill. Both Zewail and Sacar are naturalized U.S. citizens.

Dan Shechtman, Chemistry 2011, explaining the atomic structure of quasicrystals, in 1985, at a meeting of the U.S. National Institute of Standards and Technology

Then there's Israel. Although the nation is geographically in Asia, all of the Israeli honorands are of European Ashkenazi parentage.

Created a half century after the Nobel Prize was first awarded, Israel can already claim six science laureates, placing it among nations with the highest number of Nobel science prizes on a per capita basis. The Israelis are all 21st century prizewinners, considering that the country has only been in existence since 1948, and that the average age of science laureates is close to sixty years old. Four science laureates were born in Israel—Aaron Ciechanover[C] (2004), Ada Yonath* (2009), Dan Shechtman[C] (2011), and Arieh Warshel[C] (2013). Avram Hershko[C] (2004) is of Hungarian birth. Michael Levitt[C] (2013), born in South Africa, moved to Israel when he was 21 years old and acquired citizenship there.

EXHIBIT IV
JEWISH NOBEL PRIZEWINNERS–
PLACE OF BIRTH AND NATIONALITY

Names in **bold** are U.S. citizens by birth or naturalization.

Last Name, First Name	Nobel Prize, Year	Place of Birth	Nationality
Abrikosov, Alexei	Physics, 2003	Moscow, Russia/ USSR	Russian
Alferov, Zhores	Physics, 2000	Vitebsk, Belarus/USSR	Russian/USA
Altman, Sidney	Chemistry, 1989	Montreal, Canada	Canadian/USA
Ashkin, Arthur	Physics, 2018	Brooklyn, NY	USA
Axel, Richard	Medicine, 2004	Brooklyn, NY	USA
Axelrod, Julius	Medicine, 1970	New York, NY	USA
Baeyer, Adolph von	Chemistry, 1905	Berlin, Germany	German
Baltimore, David	Medicine, 1975	New York, NY	USA
Barany, Robert	Medicine, 1914	Vienna, Austria	Austrian/Swedish
Barish, Barry	Physics, 2017	Omaha, Nebraska	USA
Benacerraf, Baruj	Medicine, 1980	Caracas, Venezuela	Venezuelan/USA
Berg, Paul	Chemistry, 1980	New York, NY	USA
Bethe, Hans	Physics, 1967	Strasbourg, Germany	German/USA
Beutler, Bruce	Medicine, 2011	Chicago, IL	USA
Bloch, Felix	Physics, 1952	Zurich, Switzerland	Swiss/USA
Bloch, Konrad	Medicine, 1964	Neisse, Germany	German/USA
Blumberg, Baruch	Medicine, 1976	Brooklyn, NY	USA
Bohr, Niels	Physics, 1922	Copenhagen, Denmark	Danish/USA

Last Name, First Name	Nobel Prize, Year	Place of Birth	Nationality
Born, Max	Physics, 1954	Breslau, Germany	German/British
Brenner, Sydney	Medicine, 2002	Germiston, So. Africa	British
Brown, Herbert	Chemistry, 1979	London, England	British/USA
Brown, Michael	Medicine, 1985	New York, NY	USA
Calvin, Melvin	Chemistry, 1961	St. Paul, MN	USA
Chain, Sir Ernst	Medicine, 1945	Berlin, Germany	German/British
Chalfie, Martin	Chemistry, 2008	Chicago, IL	USA
Charpak, Georges	Physics, 1992	Dubrovica, Poland	Polish/French
Ciechanover, Aaron	Chemistry, 2004	Haifa, Palestine	Israeli
Cohen, Stanley	Medicine, 1986	Brooklyn, NY	USA
Cohen-Tannoudji, Claude	Physics, 1997	Constantine, Algeria	French
Cooper, Leon	Physics, 1972	New York, NY	USA
Cori, Gerty Radnitz	Medicine, 1947	Prague, Austria-Hungary	Czech/USA
Edelman, Gerald	Medicine, 1972	New York, NY	USA
Ehrlich, Paul	Medicine, 1908	Strehlen, Prussia	German
Einstein, Albert	Physics, 1921	Ulm, Germany	German/Swiss/USA
Elion, Gertrude	Medicine, 1988	New York, NY	USA
Englert, Francois	Physics, 2013	Etterbeck, Belgium	Belgian
Erlanger, Joseph	Medicine, 1944	San Francisco, CA	USA
Feynman, Richard	Physics, 1965	New York, NY	USA
Fire, Andrew	Medicine, 2006	Palo Alto, CA	USA

Last Name, First Name	Nobel Prize, Year	Place of Birth	Nationality
Fischer, Edmond	Medicine, 1992	Shanghai, China	Swiss/USA
Franck, James	Physics, 1925	Hamburg, Germany	German
Frank, Ilya	Physics, 1958	Leningrad, Russia	Russian
Friedman, Jerome	Physics, 1990	Chicago, IL	USA
Furchgott, Robert	Medicine, 1998	Charleston, SC	USA
Gabor, Dennis	Physics, 1971	Budapest, Hungary	Hungarian/British
Gasser, Herbert	Medicine, 1944	Platteville, WI	USA
Gell-Mann, Murray	Physics, 1969	New York, NY	USA
Gilbert, Walter	Chemistry, 1980	Boston, MA	USA
Gilman, Alfred	Medicine, 1994	New Haven, CT	USA
Ginzburg, Vitaly	Physics, 2003	Moscow, Russia/USSR	Russian
Glaser, Donald	Physics, 1960	Cleveland, OH	USA
Glashow, Sheldon	Physics, 1979	New York, NY	USA
Glauber, Roy	Physics, 2005	New York, NY	USA
Goldstein, Joseph	Medicine, 1985	Sumter, SC	USA
Greengard, Paul	Medicine, 2000	New York, NY	USA
Gross, David	Physics, 2004	Washington, DC	USA
Haber, Fritz	Chemistry, 1918	Breslau, Germany	German
Haroche, Serge	Chemistry, 2012	Casablanca, Morocco	French
Hauptman, Herbert	Chemistry, 1985	Bronx, NY	USA
Heeger, Alan	Chemistry, 2000	Sioux City, IA	USA
Hersko, Avram	Chemistry, 2004	Karcag, Hungary	Hungarian/Israeli
Hertz, Gustav	Physics, 1925	Hamburg, Germany	German

Last Name, First Name	Nobel Prize, Year	Place of Birth	Nationality
Hevesy, George de	Chemistry, 1943	Budapest, Austria-Hungary	Hungarian/ Swedish
Hoffmann, Roald	Chemistry, 1981	Zloczow, Poland	Polish/USA
Hofstadter, Robert	Physics, 1961	New York, NY	USA
Horvitz, H. Robert	Medicine, 2002	Chicago, IL	USA
Jacob, Francois	Medicine, 1965	Nancy, France	French
Josephson, Brian	Physics, 1973	Cardiff, Wales, U.K.	British
Kandel, Eric	Medicine, 2000	Vienna, Austria	Austrian/USA
Kapitsa, Pyotr	Physics, 1978	Kronstadt, Russia	Russian
Karle, Jerome	Chemistry, 1985	Brooklyn, NY	USA
Karplus, Martin	Chemistry, 2013	Vienna, Austria	Austrian/USA
Katz, Sir Bernard	Medicine, 1970	Leipzig, Germany	German/British
Klug, Sir Aaron	Chemistry, 1982	Želvas, Lithuania	Lithuanian/British
Kohn, Walter	Chemistry, 1998	Vienna, Austria	Austrian/USA
Kornberg, Arthur	Medicine, 1959	Brooklyn, NY	USA
Kornberg, Roger	Chemistry, 2006	St. Louis, MO	USA
Kosterlitz, J. Michael	Physics, 2016	Aberdeen, Scotland	UK/USA
Krebs, Sir Hans	Medicine, 1953	Hildesheim, Germany	German/British
Kroto, Sir Harold	Chemistry, 1996	Cambridgeshire, England	British
Landau, Lev	Physics, 1962	Baku, Azerbaijan, Russia	Russian
Landsteiner, Karl	Medicine, 1930	Vienna, Austria	Austrian/USA
Lederberg, Joshua	Medicine, 1958	Montclair, NJ	USA

Last Name, First Name	Nobel Prize, Year	Place of Birth	Nationality
Lederman, Leon	Physics, 1988	New York, NY	USA
Lee, David	Physics, 1996	Rye, NY	USA
Lefkowitz, Robert	Physics, 2012	New York, NY	USA
Levi-Montalcini, Rita	Medicine, 1986	Turin, Italy	Italian/USA
Levitt, Michael	Chemistry, 2013	Pretoria, South Africa	British/Israeli/USA
Lipmann, Fritz	Medicine, 1953	Koningsberg, Prussia	German/USA
Lippmann, Gabriel	Physics, 1908	Holerich, Luxembourg	French
Loewi, Otto	Medicine, 1936	Frankfurt, Germany	German/USA
Luria, Salvador	Medicine, 1969	Turin, Italy	Italian/USA
Lwoff, Andre	Medicine, 1965	Allier, France	French
Marcus, Rudolph	Chemistry, 1992	Montreal, Canada	Canadian/USA
Metchnikoff, Ilya	Medicine, 1908	Kharkov, Russia	Russian
Meyerhof, Otto	Medicine, 1922	Hannover, Germany	German/USA
Michelson, Albert	Physics, 1907	Strelno, Prussia	German/USA
Milstein, Cesar	Medicine, 1984	Bahia Blanca, Argentina	Argentinian/ British
Moissan, Henri	Chemistry, 1906	Paris, France	French
Mottelson, Benjamin	Physics, 1975	Chicago, IL	USA/Danish
Muller, Hermann	Medicine, 1946	New York, NY	USA
Müller, Karl A.	Physics, 1987	Basel, Switzerland	Swiss
Nathans, Daniel	Medicine, 1978	Wilmington, DE	USA
Nirenberg, Marshall	Medicine, 1968	New York, NY	USA

Last Name, First Name	Nobel Prize, Year	Place of Birth	Nationality
Olah, George	Chemistry, 1994	Budapest, Hungary	Hungarian/USA
Osheroff, Douglas	Physics, 1996	Aberdeen, WA	USA
Pauli, Wolfgang	Physics, 1945	Vienna, Austria	Austrian/Swiss
Penzias, Arno	Physics, 1978	Munich, Germany	German/USA
Perl, Martin	Physics, 1995	New York, NY	USA
Perlmutter, Saul	Physics, 2011	Champaign, IL	USA
Perutz, Max	Chemistry, 1962	Vienna, Austria	Austrian/British
Polanyi, John	Chemistry, 1986	Berlin, Germany	German/Canadian
Politzer, David	Physics, 2004	New York, NY	USA
Prigogine, Ilya	Chemistry, 1977	Moscow, Russia	Russian/Belgian
Prusiner, Stanley	Medicine, 1997	Des Moines, IA	USA
Rabi, Isidor	Physics, 1944	Rymanov, Austria-Hungary	Polish/USA
Reichstein, Tadeusz	Medicine, 1950	Wloclawek, Poland	Polish/Swiss
Reines, Frederick	Physics, 1995	Patterson, NJ	USA
Richter, Burton	Physics, 1976	Brooklyn, NY	USA
Riess, Adam	Physics, 2011	Washington, DC	USA
Rodbell, Martin	Medicine, 1994	Baltimore, MD	USA
Rosbash, Michael	Medicine, 2107	Kansas City, MO	USA
Rose, Irwin	Chemistry, 2004	Brooklyn, NY	USA
Rothman, James	Medicine, 2013	Haverhill, MA	USA
Schawlow, Arthur	Physics, 1981	Mt. Vernon, NY	USA
Schekman, Randy	Medicine, 2013	St. Paul, MN	USA

Last Name, First Name	Nobel Prize, Year	Place of Birth	Nationality
Schwartz, Melvin	Physics, 1988	New York, NY	USA
Schwinger, Julian	Physics, 1965	New York, NY	USA
Segrè, Emilio	Physics, 1959	Rome, Italy	Italian/USA
Shechtman, Daniel	Chemistry, 2011	Tel Aviv, Palestine	Israeli
Stein, William	Chemistry, 1972	New York, NY	USA
Steinberger, Jack	Physics, 1988	Bad Kissingen, Germany	German/USA
Steinman, Ralph	Medicine, 2011	Montreal, Canada	Canadian
Stern, Otto	Physics, 1943	Soran, Germany	German/USA
Temin, Howard	Medicine, 1975	Philadelphia, PA	USA
Vane, Sir John	Medicine, 1982	Tardebigg, England	British
Varmus, Harold	Medicine, 1989	Oceanside, NY	USA
Waksman, Selman	Medicine, 1952	Priluka, Ukraine, Russia	Russian/USA
Wald, George	Medicine, 1967	New York, NY	USA
Wallach, Otto	Chemistry, 1910	Konigsberg, Prussia	German
Warburg, Otto	Medicine, 1931	Freiburg, Germany	German
Warshel, Arieh	Chemistry, 2103	Kibbutz in Palestine	Israeli/USA
Weinberg, Steven	Physics, 1979	New York, NY	USA
Weiss, Rainer	Physics, 2017	Berlin, Germany	German/USA
Wigner, Eugene	Physics, 1963	Budapest, Hungary	Hungarian/USA
Willstatter, Richard	Chemistry, 1915	Karlsruhe, Germany	German/Swiss
Yalow, Rosalyn	Medicine, 1977	New York, NY	USA
Yonath, Ada	Chemistry, 2009	Jerusalem, British Mandate Palestine	Israeli

V. Germany's Loss,
America's Gain

Until the Second World War, Germany dominated the Nobel science awards overall. By 1940, only the 40th year of the Nobel prizes, Germany had garnered 34 science awards, with German Jews accounting for more than a third. With the advent of the Nazis, Jewish laureates and laureates-to-be fled Germany and its Axis allies, Austria, Hungary, and Italy. The outflow of talent resulted in a drastic decline in European scientific leadership. Such renowned medical centers as Vienna and Berlin lost nearly half of their physicians and the majority of their medical school faculty.

Even before Jews were fully aware of the dreadful events to come under the Nazis, there was widespread disbelief and disillusionment. By and large, they identified with and were proud of being German or Austrian. Many had served with distinction in the military in World War I. Mostly secular and often indifferent to religion, many considered themselves German or Austrian first, then Jews. They were part of these nations' vibrant cultural and intellectual life, participating extensively in music, literature, and the arts. Jewish scientists and medical doctors attended and taught in the most prestigious universities and institutions, such as the Universities of Vienna, Göttingen, Heidelberg, Berlin, Munich and the Kaiser Wilhelm Institute. The flowering of Jewish life and cultural contributions came to an abrupt halt with the rise of Nazism and was followed by vicious persecution and annihilation. Fortunately for their own survival, and to the benefit of America and the world, many top scientists were able to flee once Hitler promulgated his edicts banning Jews from universities and professions in 1933. They were able to leave while fleeing was still possible. Even those, like Hans Bethe* (Physics 1967), who did not identify themselves as Jews (though he was born to a Jewish mother), were also in jeopardy and had to leave Germany.

Showing tremendous resilience, these scientists restarted their careers, although initially at a lower level than they had left behind. Unlike the closed doors to immigration encountered by ordinary Jews seeking to enter the United States, renowned Jewish scientists, as well as other scientists fleeing fascism, were able to find refuge primarily in the U.S. and in Great Britain. Their professional reputations and established relationships with eminent scientists abroad saved them.

Some who could not leave themselves had the foresight to have their children escape. In 1934, when Jack Steinberger* (Physics 1988) was only thirteen years old, his parents sent him and his brother from Germany to live with a foster family in Chicago. As late as 1939 the parents of Arno Penzias[P] (Physics 1978) and Walter Kohn[C‡] (Chemistry 1998), from Munich and Vienna, respectively, were able to send their children on the "*kindertransport*" to England. The *kindertransport* was a unique humanitarian operation that rescued children in peril before the outbreak of WWII. Some 10,000 mostly Jewish children were placed in British foster homes. Sadly, most of these children were their families' sole survivors.

‡ Curiously, the British authorities sent Walter Kohn, then only seventeen years old, to a detention camp in Canada as an "enemy alien."

Walter Kohn with his parents and sister in Vienna, 1932

Those who fled Europe in the late 1930s to escape being rounded up and sent to the concentration camps often had harrowing experiences. Richard Willstatter* (Chemistry 1915) had turned down teaching positions abroad, deciding to stay in Germany. However, in 1938 police sought to arrest him and send him for internment in Dachau concentration camp. He tried to escape by rowing across Lake Constance to Switzerland, but was captured by the Gestapo. Through the intervention of the Swiss ambassador, he was granted asylum in Switzerland, where he remained until his death. The same year, Otto Meyerhof* (Medicine 1922) escaped Germany on a circuitous route through Switzerland, Paris, southern France, then across the Pyrenees into Spain, and finally on to the United States.

With Hitler's takeover of Austria, Otto Loewi* (Medicine 1936) was imprisoned with his family. In exchange for the award money he won with his Nobel Prize, Germany allowed him to leave for Belgium. Georges Charpak* (Physics 1992), a member of the French Resistance, was imprisoned by the German-allied Vichy government and sent to Dachau. He survived. "Luckily I was only regarded as a Pole and a terrorist. They didn't know I was a Jew."[13]

Otto Warburg* (Medicine 1931) of Jewish parentage (father) remained in Germany. Although demoted and shunned he was allowed to continue his cancer research because it was of great personal concern to Hitler. To this end Hermann Goering classified Warburg as less than one-quarter Jewish, which was sufficient to save his life. Gustav Hertz (Physics 1925), who also had a Jewish father, had been a German officer in World War I. In 1934 he was forced to resign from the Technical University of Berlin, but somehow managed to continue working on atomic physics at the industrial giant Siemens. In 1945, along with

Georges Charpak as a young man

13 Schwarzschild, Bertram. "Nobel Physics Prize Goes to Charpak for Inventing Particle Detectors." *Physics Today* Jan. 1993

hundreds of German scientists from the Soviet-occupied zone, he moved to the Soviet Union, where he continued his research. He returned to Germany in 1955 as a physics professor at the University of Leipzig in Soviet-occupied East Germany. He remained there until his retirement in 1967.

Not directly affected by Nazism, the Russian Jewish science Nobelists of the period—Ilya Frank[P], Lev Landau,* Pyotr Kapitsa,* Vitaly Ginzberg,* Zhores Alferov,* and Alexei Abrisokov[P]—all of whom remained working in the Soviet Union. Selman Waksman* and Ilya Prigogine,* both Russian-born, emigrated with their parents when they were children.

A considerable number of foreign born U.S. science Nobel prizewinners were Hitler-era German Jewish émigré scientists. The United States reaped the giant share of these scientists with England a distant second destination. Five of these British Jewish immigrants were knighted "Sir" by Queen Elizabeth II—Ernst Chain[M] (Medicine 1945), Hans Krebs* (Medicine 1953), Bernard Katz[M] (Medicine 1970), and Aaron Klug[C] (Chemistry 1982), as well as Harold Kroto* (Chemistry 1996), who, while British born, was the son of refugees from Nazi Germany.

The Nobel science laureates and laureates-to-be were only the most visible elite. Hundreds of lesser-known scientists also sought refuge, mostly in the United States. These displaced scientists, Christians as well as Jews, found a hospitable environment and the resources required to continue their work. Their contributions helped the United States become the dominant country in science after World War II. Beyond their own contributions, these immigrant scientists had a multiplier effect through training a new generation of scientists, some of whom became Nobel prizewinners themselves.

The impact of Germany's loss and America's gain was nowhere more evident than in the so-called "Manhattan Project." Several of the refugee scientists, who had worked on some aspect of nuclear fission in Germany, were concerned that the U.S. was falling behind and feared that Germany could develop the atomic bomb first, giving it a decisive weapon in a military confrontation. A group of these scientists asked Albert Einstein,* the most prestigious physicist among them, to write to President Franklin D. Roosevelt urging him to take action. Unlike most government decision-making, this drew a quick response. Only six weeks later, on October 11, 1939, President Roosevelt approved uranium research that led to the creation of the Manhattan Project and eventually resulted in the development of the atomic bomb. Hitler's invasion of Poland on September 19, 1939, which started World War II, undoubtedly hastened the decision.

The project brought the most brilliant scientists together to work for the United States' government to advance the creation of a weapon that would be decisive in a war. The group included many Jewish émigré scientists who had fled the Nazis. There was Eugene Wigner[P], a Hungarian physicist who had long worked on nuclear research in Germany, and his fellow Hungarian Jews, Edward Teller, "father of the hydrogen bomb," and Leo Szilard, who conceived of nuclear reaction. Other Jewish scientists on the project included James Franck,* Isidor Rabi[P], Felix Bloch,* Niels Bohr,* Hans Bethe,* Max Born,* and Emilio Segrè.* The well-known physicist Enrico Fermi, also part of this group, was not Jewish, but he left Europe to protect his Jewish wife.

The project's U.S.-born American Jews included J. Robert Oppenheimer, who oversaw it from beginning to end, Julian Schwinger,* Richard Feynman,* Frederick Reines[P], and Roy Glauber.* The latter, an 18-year-old Harvard sophomore, was considered so

Albert Einstein and Robert Oppenheimer at the
Institute for Advanced Study, Princeton University

brilliant that the U.S. government recruited him to work on developing atomic fission at the Los Alamos, New Mexico, site. Neither Oppenheimer nor Teller nor Szilard were awarded the Nobel Prize in physics, presumably because their work was not considered beneficial to mankind. All of the other scientists mentioned above received Nobel prizes in physics, but their awards apparently were for discoveries not directly related to the bomb.

Ironically, many of the scientists who worked on the development of the atomic bomb were also among its foremost critics. Although Einstein, a well-known pacifist, did not take part in the Manhattan Project, he used his influence to propel its creation. Together with other scientists, he strenuously opposed the proliferation of atomic weapons. James Franck* (Physics 1925) went so far as to urge the government not to use the bomb against

Japan. Initially, these scientists had feared that if the bomb were in German hands it would be used to obliterate the Allies. Once Germany was vanquished, however, and the horrors of Hiroshima and Nagasaki became apparent, many of them wanted to curb any further development of the weapon that they had helped create.

VI. The Tectonic Shift

To appreciate the scope of Jewish achievement it is helpful to understand Jewish demographics. How many Jews are there in the world? Where do they live? How accurate are the data? This is the stuff of demographics, the study of population, normally not the most electrifying subject for the average reader. In the case of the Jews, however, demographics are much more than just dry statistics. The numbers illustrate the dramatic shifts in Jewish population as a direct consequence of the Holocaust and the creation of the state of Israel.

The number of Jews worldwide, as well as in any nation, is at best a rough estimate as census information rarely includes a breakout. Even if it did, the data would still be incomplete as many Jews who identify with Judaism ethnically and culturally, but not religiously, may not respond or be counted. The estimates of Jewish population numbers vary considerably depending on the criteria used and the scope of the survey. Demographic information herein is based on data from recognized experts of American Jewish demography, Ira Sheskin (University of Miami) and Arnold Dashefsky (University of Connecticut), and Sergio Della-Pergola (Hebrew University, Jerusalem), the leading authority on world Jewish demographics.[14] They warn, "Analysts should resign

14 Sheskin, Ira and Arnold Dashefsky. Editors, *American Jewish Yearbook 2018*. Springer Nature Switzerland AG.
Della Pergola, Sergio. *American Jewish Yearbook 2018*, pages 361–447.

themselves to the paradox of the permanently provisional nature of Jewish population estimates."

The total worldwide Jewish population as of 2018 was estimated at 14.6 million by Della Pergola and 15.8 million by Sheskin and Dashefsky. The latter's estimate appears more on target based on their copious compilation of data presented in the *American Jewish Year Book 2018*. An explanation for the difference is taken up below when U.S. Jewish population is discussed. In either case, Jews comprise only one-fifth of one percent (0.2%) of the world's population.

The most startling figure is that by 2018, some 85% of all Jews lived in just two countries—Israel and the United States. Before World War II, it was estimated that there were some 16.5 million Jews; by 1945 there were 10.5 million. Demographically speaking, Jews have not fully recovered from the Holocaust. The six million Jews killed accounted for 36% of all Jews worldwide in 1940. In proportional terms, it would have been equivalent to the death of some 50 million Americans at the time. While the world's population has tripled, Jews—who accounted for 0.8% of the world's population in 1940—now make up only one-fourth of that number.

Not only has the total number of Jews decreased, but there also has been a seismic shift in where they live. Prior to the Second World War, the largest concentration of Jews by far was in Europe, with an estimated 58% of the world's Jewish population, versus less than 10% in 2018. Poland alone accounted for more than three million Jews, almost all of whom died in the Holocaust. Polish Jews now number only a few thousand, about one-tenth of one percent of the pre-World War II population. Of the 1,250,000 Jews in the Soviet Union killed during the Second World War, 90%

were from the now independent states of Ukraine and Belarus. In three other countries, Hungary, Romania, and Czechoslovakia, nearly a million died. The combined Jewish population in these countries in 2016 was estimated at 60,000 (mostly in Hungary). As for Germany, the Jewish population in 1933 was 550,000 versus 34,000 in 1980. By 2018, it had increased to 116,000, owing largely to immigrants from the former Soviet Union/Russia. Berlin was one of the fastest-growing Jewish communities outside of Israel.

Currently, France ranks third after the U.S. and Israel as home to Jews, with 2.9%. Other significant Jewish populations are in Canada (2.5%), United Kingdom (1.9%), and Russia/Ukraine (1.5%). Rounding out the top ten are Argentina, Australia, Germany, and Brazil. As recently as 1980, the U.S.S.R./Russia accounted for almost 10%, but when Russian Jews were allowed to leave in the 1990s, a mass emigration ensued—mostly to Israel. The U.S. and Canada are the only countries apart from Israel where Jews make up at least 1% of the population.

The Jewish population of Israel as of 2018 was estimated at 6,560,000, 74% of the population of the country. In 1938, some 400,000 Jews lived in the British Mandate of Palestine, which represented only 2.5% of world Jewry at the time. The seismic movement in Jewish population is attributable to two magna events—the Holocaust and the founding of the State of Israel. Following World War II, and after the independence of Israel in 1948, the population grew rapidly, principally from the inflow of Holocaust survivors. For most of the displaced survivors, returning to their homes in Central and Eastern Europe was not an option. Many of their countrymen had collaborated with the Nazis. Others remained hostile to their return to their homelands, especially when it came to reclaiming their now-occupied homes.

At the same time, Jews who wanted to immigrate, preferably to the United States, were effectively kept out by quota restrictions.

Sephardic and Mizrahi Jews expelled from North Africa and the Middle East countries made up another major influx into Israel. An estimated 900,000 Jews lived in the Arab/Muslim world in the mid 1940s. The ensuing hostility of Arab nations following the independence of the State of Israel led to an exodus, mostly to Israel, of Jews who had lived in these lands for hundreds, if not thousands, of years: 290,000 Jews left Morocco, 53,000 left Tunisia, 26,000 were expelled from Algeria, 37,000 were forced to leave from each Egypt and Libya, 130,000 fled Iraq, 52,000 left Yemen, and 14,000 departed from Syria and Lebanon.[15] These countries' Jewish communities no longer exist or are but remnants of their former selves. Their descendants now surpass the number of Israelis who are of European (Ashkenazi) origin.

The United States is home to some 44% of all Jews. The only time the U.S. Census Bureau surveyed religion as a category was in 1957, and the census does not classify Jews as an ethnic group. Current estimates of the number of Jews in the United States rely on surveys of local Jewish communities, Jewish organizations, and academic demographers and universities. In determining Jewish population, non-religious, non-practicing ethnic Jews are normally counted along with those who are formally affiliated. The difference between the demographers' estimates of total world Jewish population is due to the U.S. estimate. Della-Pergola's estimate of 5,700,000 is based on what he terms core Jews, while Sheskin and Dashefsky have a somewhat broader and more realistic definition which increases the number to

---

15 *Forgotten Exodus*, World Jewish Congress, New York.

6,900,000. In either case, the percentage of American Jews of the U.S. population remains about 2%.

There is a marked geographical concentration of American Jews: As many as 43% live in just two states, New York and California. Add Florida and New Jersey and the total is almost 60%. Other states with large Jewish populations are Illinois, Pennsylvania, Massachusetts, and Maryland/D.C. These eight states are home to 77% of all American Jews.

The concentration is even more pronounced if we hone in on the expanded urban metropolitan areas with their environs—New York City, Los Angeles, and Southeast Florida's coastal strip account for the residence of almost half of all American Jews. Include the metropolitan areas of San Francisco, Chicago, Philadelphia, Boston, and Washington/Baltimore and three out of four American Jews live in these urban areas.

The New York City mega-metropolitan area—defined to include its vast commuter communities in Northeastern New Jersey, Long Island, Westchester and Fairfield counties—is likely to be home to one out of three American Jews. Furthermore, it is probable that one out of seven Jews in the world may reside in this area. It is not surprising, then, that this concentration is reflected in the number of Jewish American Nobel science prizewinners—more than a third of whom were born just in New York City itself.

VII. Women Nobelists

How many women have won a Nobel Prize in science? How did female scientists fare in comparison to their male counterparts? Of the total of 607 Nobel prizes in science awarded through 2018, only twenty (3.3%) were awarded to 19 women (Marie Curie won two). In the Nobel Prize's first 100 years, only ten women received the distinction. It wasn't until 1977 that the first U.S. born woman, Rosalyn Sussman Yalow,* won a Nobel prize in the sciences. The good news, however, is that the pace has been accelerating. In the years since 2004, there already have been nine women science laureates, almost matching the number of awards to women in the entire previous century.

The significant under-representation of women among Nobel science award winners undoubtedly reflects the longstanding gender discrimination in education and professions. Having relatively few women in visible positions in science puts them at a disadvantage when it comes to being recognized. At the same time, the Nobel Science Committees' members and nominators are overwhelmingly male. As for the non-science laureates, only one woman has ever received the Economics award. Women have been considerably more prominent, however, in the other two Nobel categories, literature and peace awards, notably the former.

In the mid 1990s, a M.I.T. (Massachusetts Institute of Technology) committee concluded that the marginalization of female scientists at M.I.T. "was often accompanied by differences in salary, space, awards, resources, and response to outside offers between men and women faculty, with women receiving less despite professional accomplishments equal to those of their (male) colleagues."[16] Generally speaking, women have made impressive gains. It is not uncommon for half of all university students to be female, and women doctors and lawyers are commonplace. Still the "glass ceiling" persists in science as well as in other fields.

Lawrence Summers, then President of Harvard University, caused quite a stir in 2005 with remarks he made about women in science. At a private conference about women and minorities in science and engineering, he suggested that perhaps the under representation of women among scientists, engineers, and mathematicians may stem more from innate differences in scientific aptitude between men and women and less from gender discrimination. His statement caused a furor among the largely female audience and received wide dissemination. The controversy that resulted from his remarks was an important factor contributing to his forced resignation as President of Harvard.

Nine of the nineteen women honorands are Americans (three naturalized citizens) and five are Jewish. Awards in medicine predominate. Like their fellow male honorands, Jewish women account for about one out of four female science prizewinners worldwide and more than half of the American women Nobelists. The first woman to win a Nobel Prize in science, and undoubtedly the best known, was Polish-born French scientist Marie Sklodowska Curie, who received the prize just three years after it was first awarded. Not only that, she is the only person to have received awards in two different fields of science—physics

16 Pollack, Eileen. *The New York Times Magazine. The New York Times,* 5 Oct. 2013.

in 1903, shared with her husband Pierre, and chemistry in 1911. Their daughter, Irene Joliot-Curie (Chemistry 1935), was the second woman to be honored also jointly with her husband Frederic Joliot. Five Nobel science prizes between parents and children is an unparalleled feat.

The first U.S. citizen (naturalized) to be awarded a Nobel prize in science, as well as the first Jewish woman, was Gerty Radnitz Cori* (Medicine 1947). As in the case of the Curie family, she received the award jointly with her husband Carl Cori. Both were born in Prague in the same year, 1896, and later emigrated to the United States. The Coris had the same educational background—they were actually university classmates —and were lifelong professional collaborators. In spite of this, in marked contrast to her husband, Gerty Cori initially had difficulties obtaining even junior research positions, and when she did receive a senior appointment, it was at a lower compensation.

Marie Curie

Rita Levi-Montalcini* (Medicine 1986), born in Italy in 1909, faced the prevalent attitude about a woman's role at the time. Her traditional Italian father objected to her career ambitions because he believed that a professional career would conflict with her duties as wife and mother. In spite of her father's objections, Levi-Montalcini obtained a medical degree and had an illustrious professional career. She never married because she thought it would interfere with her work to which she was totally devoted. "I never had any hesitation or regret in this sense," she said in 2006.[17] Levi-Montalcini also had the distinction of being the oldest surviving Nobel prizewinner in any category ever. She died in Rome in 2013 at the age of 103.

Rita Levi-Montalcini in her lab at Washington University of St. Louis, Becker School of Medicine

Gertrude Elion* (Medicine 1988), like other female honorands born in the early decades of the 1900s, found it difficult to be a scientist in what was then a man's world. She succeeded due to her tenacity in spite of economic, social, and gender barriers. Not having the funds to attend graduate school, she sought a lab job. In her autobiography she noted, "The few positions that existed in laboratories were not available to women. By chance I met a chemist who was looking for a laboratory assistant, although he was unable to pay me a salary at the time. I decided that the experience would be worthwhile."[18]

---

17 *Miami Herald* 31 Dec. 2012, "Rita Levi-Montalcini obituary."

18 "Gertrude B. Elion—Biographical." Nobel Prize.org

Later, she was able to attend New York University where she was the only female in her class to receive a degree in chemistry. Although scientific jobs in industry were essentially closed to women, she managed to secure a position with Burroughs Wellcome Research Laboratories, a pharmaceutical company. Elion never married. She believed that it was not possible to devote herself fully to both a career and a family. Elion felt sufficiently rewarded by the impact of the drugs she helped develop to alleviate human suffering—medications for the immune system, leukemia, gout, herpes, shingles, and AIDS.

In contrast to the two previously mentioned honorands, Rosalyn Yalow* (Medicine 1977) was deeply engaged professionally, yet she successfully managed to balance her professional work with her life as wife, mother and homemaker—even keeping a kosher kitchen. Yalow was the first woman to receive an undergraduate degree in physics from Hunter College in New York and the only woman out of a class of 400 at the School of Engineering of the University of Illinois. She was an inspiration to woman of her generation seeking to have both careers and families.

Ada Yonath,* née Lifshitz, was the first Israeli woman to win a Nobel Prize (Chemistry 2009) in science and the first woman in 45 years to win Nobel Prize in chemistry. She overcame many obstacles. Yonath was born into a poor, religious family of Polish immigrants who had very little formal education. Her father, who was chronically ill, died when she was eleven. Yonath had to work to help the family subsist. Nevertheless, through sheer determination and hard work she managed to obtain an undergraduate degree and a M.S. at Hebrew University in Jerusalem and a doctorate at the Weizmann Institute. Yonath was married and had a daughter.

To round off the list of all women science laureates:

- Maria Goeppert Mayer (Physics 1963), a German-born naturalized American

- Dorothy Crowfoot Hodgkin (Chemistry 1964), British

- Barbara McClintock (Medicine 1983), American

- Christiane Nusslein-Volhard (Medicine 1995), German

- Linda Buck (Medicine 2004), American

- Francoise Barre-Sinoussi (Medicine 2008), French

- Carol Greinder (Medicine 2009), American

- Elizabeth Blackburn (Medicine 2009), Australian

- May Brit-Moser (Medicine 2014), Norwegian

- Youyou Tu (Medicine 2015), Chinese

- Donna Strickland (Physics 2018), Canadian—She became the first woman in fifty-five years to win an award in physics.

- Frances H. Arnold (Chemistry 2018), American

VIII. Science & Religion

Religion and nationality have historically been interlinked, imposed on a nation or geographical entity by the ruler, be it Emperor, King or Prince. In general, if one is Italian, Austrian, or Spanish, one is most likely Roman Catholic; if English, most likely Anglican; if Scandinavian, Protestant; if Russian, Russian Orthodox; if Egyptian or Pakistani, Muslim; and so on. The United States is a different story—a mixed bag of religions.

The founding fathers promulgated a remarkably forward-looking concept: The US was founded as a secular nation with the separation of church and state. The founders broke with the European tradition of commingling the authority of the state and church in order to create a freer, less authoritarian society. The wisdom of the foresight of the founding fathers is evident in the political, economic, and industrial evolution of the United States. In contrast, President John Adams expressed pessimism about the possibility of democracy in Latin America because in Spain and Portugal church and state were intertwined to such a degree that "a free government and the Roman Catholic religion can never exist together."[19]

When addressing question of the religious affiliations or denominations of Nobel science laureates, the information often is not

19 Peterson, Merrill D. *Adams and Jefferson: A Revolutionary Dialogue.* Mercer University Lamar Memorial Lecture Series (1975) Athens, Georgia: University of Georgia Press, 1976, p. 118

available. The usual assumption is that religion is passed on by parents. When there appears to be no record in biographical research, the science laureate's religion is generally reported as "unknown," "of Protestant background," or "probably Christian." Protestants have received Nobel science awards more or less in accordance to their proportion of the population, while Catholics are under-represented relative to their number. Among Protestants, there is a marked predominance of the more traditional denominations, such as Anglican for the English, Episcopalian and Presbyterian for Americans, and Lutheran for Germans. There appears to be a dearth of laureates who adhere to fundamentalist or evangelical beliefs. Besides the Jews, the minuscule non-denominational Unitarians are also greatly over-represented.

Throughout the ages, science and religion have been in conflict. While science relies on reason and data for its burden of proof, religion is based on unsubstantiated faith. Historically speaking, refuting some tenets of the Catholic Church was a punishable offense that could even result in being burned at the stake. Accused by the Inquisition of heresy for his thesis that the Earth revolves around the sun (not vice versa), Galileo had to recant in order to save his life. Sir Isaac Newton, who was born into an Anglican family, eschewed religion, but hid his views during his entire life to avoid repercussions. While such drastic actions are long gone, the mind-set has lingered on.

Scientists are generally skeptical and do not want to get embroiled in religious discussions. Even as late as the twentieth century, it still was necessary to at least give lip service to conventional religion, as atheism and non-belief were universally shunned. As a practical matter, those who were hostile to atheism were in positions to hinder scientists' progress in various ways. They could block university admissions, research grants, faculty appointments,

VIII. Science & Religion

employment opportunities, membership in professional groups, and the receipt of awards.

What we do know about many laureates' religious views, as differentiated from their inherited birth affiliation, is usually gleaned from their own writings and comments they made or that others recorded. Nobel prizewinners in science, whatever their family's religion, have been predominantly secular. Some scientists' views on religion changed over time, but rarely toward embracing faith. There is a wide range of views about organized religion, from those who are just disinterested to rabid atheists. In his book, *Genius Talk: Conversations with Nobel Scientists and Other Luminaries*, covering the religious views of mainly Christian-born scientists, Denis Brian concluded that there are "few who aren't out and out atheists."[20]

Early scientists breaking with conventional religion included Thomas Edison, the prolific American inventor. His views on religion could be summarized by "Nature made us—nature did it all—not the gods of religion,"[21] but he did not want to be labelled an atheist. Catholic-raised Marie Curie, her husband, daughter, and son-in-law (Nobel science laureates all) were daring for their time by being openly anti-clerical. Few have been as stridently against religion as eminent scientists Richard Dawkins, author of *The God Delusion*, and Stephen Hawking, author of *The Grand Design*.

Among the science laureates who have expressed passionate anti-religion views publicly and in their writings and are Paul Dirac (Physics 1933) and Sir Harold Kroto* (Chemistry 1996).

---

20 Brian, Denis. *Genius Talks: Conversations with Nobel Scientists and Other Luminaries,* New York: Plenum Press, 1995, p. 242.

21 *New York Times Magazine,* 10/2/1910

Dirac, a distinguished Swiss-British Catholic physicist and a founder of the field of quantum mechanics, declared: "I cannot understand why we idle discussing religion. If we are honest, we must admit that religion is a jungle of false assertions with no basis in reality. The very idea of God is a product of human imagination."[22] In his auto-biography, Kroto wrote extensively about his views on religion: "I am a devout atheist—nothing else makes any sense to me...At no point do I remember taking religion seriously or even feeling that biblical stories were different from fairy tales. Cer-tainly none of it made any sense...

Paul Dirac

(there is) incontrovertible evidence that no divine mystical cre-ator, other than the simple laws of nature, exists."[23]

Albert Einstein, the most renowned scientist of the twentieth century, gave a great deal of thought to the subject and had a more nuanced view of religion. He made different statements at various times in his life. In 1929, he expressed a frequently quoted view of God in cosmic and impersonal terms: "I believe in Spino-za's God, who reveals himself in the orderly harmony of all that exists, but not in a God who concerns himself with the fate and the doings of mankind."[24] Later in his life, he stated that he was agnostic, but not an atheist. However, in 1955, one year before

22. Heisenberg, Werner. *Physics and Beyond: Encounters and Conversations*, World Perspectives Series, Vol. 42. New York: Harper & Row, 1971, pp. 85–86

23. "Sir Harold Kroto—Biographical." Nobelprize.org.

24. Isaacson, Walter. *Einstein: His Life and Universe*. New York: Simon & Schuster, 2007, pp. 388–389.

his death, Einstein stated in a letter to his philosopher friend Eric Gutkind, head of the Humanist Association: "The word God for me is nothing more than the expression and product of human weakness, the Bible a collection of honorable, but still primitive legends which are nevertheless pretty childish."[25] This so-called "God letter" was auctioned at Christie's and sold for almost three million dollars.[26]

Albert Einstein

A survey the U.S. Academy of Sciences conducted among its 517 members in 1998 indicated that a great majority of all Nobel science laureates tended to be secular and non-religious. Only 7% of those surveyed expressed a belief in a personal God, 72% did not, while 20% said they were agnostic. This survey largely replicates surveys conducted in 1914 and 1933.[27] There appears to be an inverse relationship between strongly held religious beliefs and scientific achievement.

The dogma of religion constrains the mind and hampers critical thinking. Religiosity tends to encourage conformity and acceptance of the status quo. It does not put a premium on new ideas or questioning existing ones. A belief in a life in the hereafter, sometimes linked to future rewards, may further weaken motivation

---

25. Randerson, James. "Childish Superstition: Einstein's Letter." *The Guardian* [London] 13 May 2008

26 Bennett-Smith, Meredith. "Einstein 'God Letter' Sold on eBay for Just Over $3 Million." *The Huffington Post*. TheHuffingtonPost.com, 24 Oct. 2012

27 Larson, Edward J., and Witham, Larry. "Leading scientists still reject God." *Nature* 23 July 1998

to achieve in the here and now. Religious tradition may also shed light on why, with more than one 1.8 billion adherents worldwide, Muslims have only obtained a few Nobel science prizes. And those who did left their countries of origin to study and/or live in the United States or England. In his book about Arabs in the modern world, Milton Viorst noted, "Islam succeeded where Christianity failed in shackling man's power of reasoning. It was a success for which Muslim society has continued to pay heavily."[28]

A look back at family religious background of Jewish science laureates in particular reveals a generally marked difference between those from Central and Western European and those of Eastern European or Russian origin. The former tended to be secularly oriented and minimally observant. On the other hand, Eastern European Jews were more likely to be traditionally conservative in their outlook. Nonetheless, the children of these immigrants, brought up in the United States, came to have pretty much the same incidence of non-belief and level achievement. Ultra-Orthodox Jews present a sharp contrast to less religious Jews in cultural values and outlook. Other than studying the Torah and Talmud, education has not been a top priority. Technology, the pursuit of wealth, and secular achievement are largely eschewed.

Jewish Nobelists are more likely to identify themselves as atheist or agnostic, among them: Alferov,* Axelrod,* Bethe, Bohr,* Born,* Charpak,* Cooper[P], Ehrlich,* Feynman,* Gabor,* Ginzburg,* Hauptmann[C], Hoffmann[C], Hofstadter[P], Jacob,* Katz[M], Karle[C], Kroto,* Landau,* Lederman,* Levi-Montacini,* Michelson,* H. Muller[M], Olah[C], Pauli,* Perutz[C], and Weinberg[P]. That said, there always are some exceptions. One who did not stray from his

---

28 Viorst, Milton. *Sandcastles: The Arabs in Search of the Modern World*. New York: Alfred Knopf, 1994

religious roots was Baruch Blumberg* (Medicine 1976). Brought up in an orthodox home in Brooklyn, he remained involved in his Jewish faith which guided his life. He attributed his mental discipline to the study of the Talmud. His life was a testament to his view that, "There is, in Jewish thought, this idea that if you can save a single life, you can save the whole world. Saving lives is what drew me to medicine."[29]

Even when many Jewish Nobel science laureates expressed little or no interest in Judaism as a religion, they usually identified with their fellow Jews ethnically and culturally. Moreover, many were actively committed to Jewish causes and charities. To quote Einstein: "And the Jewish people, to whom I gladly belong and with whose mentality I have deep affinity."[30] He was a founder of Hebrew University in Jerusalem and was offered the presidency of Israel. In a different time and place, Vitaly Ginzburg* (Physics 2003), a communist and outspoken atheist, was active in Jewish life in Russia. He put his personal prestige on the line to fight antisemitism and to advocate Russian support of Israel, There are exceptions, of course. Richard Feynman* (Physics 1965), who described himself as "avowed atheist," rejected any ethnic or cultural identity with the Jewish people and did not want to be included on any list based on his ethnicity. (My apologies, Mr. Feynman.)

---

29 *The New York Times*, 6 Apr. 2011 Segelken, Roger H. "Baruch Blumberg, Who Discovered and Tackled Hepatitis B, Dies at 85."

30 Isaacson, Walter. *Einstein: His Life and Universe*. New York: Simon & Schuster, 2007

IX. Laureates' University Affiliations

In the earlier years of the Nobel prizes, prior to the Nazis' ascent to power, American universities did not play a role in the educational formation of the then dominant European laureates and laureates-to-be, whether Christian or Jewish. These Nobel science prizewinners often attended prestigious European universities in Berlin, Munich, Göttingen, and Heidelberg in Germany; Vienna in Austria; Zurich in Switzerland; Cambridge and Oxford in England; and the Sorbonne in Paris.

Although not educated at U.S. universities, the laureates who fled Europe after Hitler's takeover later became associated with U.S. institutions where they became professors and conducted award-winning research. The exodus was not limited to Jews. Many other scientists who opposed the Nazi and fascists regimes also chose to leave Europe. The émigré Nobel prizewinners and laureates-to-be sought refuge primarily in the United States, but also in England. They were the fortunate ones who usually obtained faculty or research appointments with American universities, although initially at lower levels than their previously held positions in Europe. These Jewish scientists were able to gain entry into the U.S. based on their professional reputations and recommendations from their American associates and fellow émigré scientists who preceded them. Ordinary Jews had no such recourse and were largely shut out of the U.S. by immigration laws and quotas.

Universities, like nations, are all too happy to claim Nobel prize-winners as their own, whether as faculty members or alumni. This brings up the question: Which American universities have the most connections with Jewish science laureates? Not an easy matter to determine. Alumni can be classified by those who have received B.S./B.A. undergraduate degrees, Master's degrees, conducted postgraduate or postdoctoral research, or obtained advanced degrees (Ph.D. or M.D.). Faculty members can be classified as current, former, or visiting. The many distinct levels of university affiliations make meaningful rankings difficult. What counts most and what weight should be given to each?

There is a lack of uniformity in the way Nobel faculty affiliations are reported. The Nobel Foundation indicates scientists' university association at the time of receiving the award. Universities prepare their own lists which vary widely. Some universities include Nobel faculty members no matter how brief their stay, such as visiting professors. Most laureates have served on the faculties of several universities and their seminal work for which they were awarded the Nobel Prize often occurred during their tenures at different universities.

The exhibit at the end of the chapter illustrates the difficulties of ranking laureates' university associations with the example of two universities, Harvard and Columbia. Historically, Columbia has been the university with the most affiliations of Jewish American scientists, followed closely by Harvard. In more recent decades, Harvard has come to the forefront. Other universities with significant participation are Massachusetts Institute of Technology (MIT), Stanford University, University of Chicago, University of California/Berkeley, New York University, and Rockefeller University—the latter a New York City-based research institution. Columbia and Harvard are also the universities where the most

Jewish Nobel science laureates earned their medical or doctorate degrees. This is also the case for faculty members.

Roy Glauber taught physics at Harvard for 60 years.

At the undergraduate level (B.S./B.A.), Columbia and Harvard head up the list for laureates-to-be, followed by CCNY (City College of New York, now CUNY [City University of New York]). The high incidence of associations of future Jewish Nobel science laureates with New York City universities—Columbia, CCNY, NYU, and Hunter College—is not surprising since so many future Jewish American laureates were born there.

CCNY ranked high in the number of undergraduate B.S. degrees, but was not a factor in graduate education or faculty. This is also understandable since it was tuition free and most readily accessible to Jewish students, especially to the children of poorer recent immigrants from Eastern Europe and Russia. Moreover, prior to the early 1950s, many universities limited the number of Jewish students they would accept for matriculation. The high concentration of Jews in the boroughs of the Bronx and Brooklyn led certain high schools to stand out in the number of laureates-to-be who attended them, notably Bronx High School of Science and Stuyvesant in Brooklyn.

When considering the university affiliations of *all* Nobel prize-winners in the sciences, Harvard clearly leads the list. Other high-ranking universities for all Nobel science awards are the University of California/Berkeley, California Institute of Technology, University of Chicago, Columbia University, Massachusetts Institute of Technology, and Stanford University. Among institutions abroad, the University of Cambridge ranks in the top tier.

Time and again one observes the pattern of interrelationship of Nobel science laureates with those who preceded them and those who followed. To cite one case out of many: Julian Schwinger* (Physics 1965) supervised the dissertations of seventy doctoral candidates, including Nobel prizewinners Roy Glauber* (Physics 2005), Walter Kohn[C] (Chemistry 1998), Sheldon Glashow[P] (Physics 1979), and Ben Mottelson[P] (Physics 1975). Schwinger, in turn, was mentored by Isidor Rabi[P] (Physics 1944), who likewise supervised many future Nobelist doctoral candidates.

Julian Schwinger: "My laboratory is my ballpoint pen."

The overwhelming majority of Jewish science laureates dedicated their lives to academic careers as university professors. Some spent practically their entire professional lives at a single university. Leon Cooper[P] (Physics 1972) has been teaching at Brown University since 1958. Other notables with four or five decades of tenure include: Roy Glauber* (Medicine 2005) and George Wald[M] (Medicine 1967), at Harvard; Melvin Calvin[C] (Chemistry 1961), University of California at Berkeley; William Stein[C] (Chemistry 1972), Rockefeller University; Eric Kandel* (Medicine 2000), Columbia; and Joseph Goldstein* (Medicine 1985), University of Texas. On the other hand, it is more common for laureates to be associated with many institutions for their education and during their careers.

At various times in their lives, some laureates divided their careers between academia, government agencies, and not-for-profit institutions. One of the most varied professional careers was that of Baruch "Barry" Blumberg* (Medicine 1976), who was associated with the N.I.H. (National Institutes of Health), two cancer research institutes, and NASA (National Aeronautics and Space Administration), as well as serving as a professor at the University of Pennsylvania and Master of Balliol College at Oxford in England.

Baruch "Barry" Blumberg

Marshall Nirenberg[M] (Medicine 1968) spent his entire career with the National Institutes of Health in Bethesda, Maryland. Other laureates who devoted large parts of their careers to the N.I.H. include Julius Axelrod* (Medicine 1970), Alfred Gilman[M] (Medicine 1994), Martin Rodbell[M] (Medicine 1994), Stanley Prusiner[M] (Medicine 1997), Andrew Fire[M] (Medicine 2006), and Harold Varmus[M] (Medicine 1989). Jerome Karle[C] and Herbert Hauptman[C] (both Chemistry 1985) were associated with the U.S. Naval Research Laboratory. Karle and his wife, also a chemist, jointly served for a total of 127 years!

Jerome Karle with the electron diffraction machine at the U.S. Naval Research Laboratory

Relatively few laureates worked in industry for corporations. Among them were Arno Penzias[P] (Physics 1978) and Arthur Schawlow[P] (Physics 1981), both of whom worked for New Jersey based Bell Laboratories, a company devoted to research and development, as did Arthur Ashkin (Physics 2018) for four decades. Gertrude Elion* (Medicine 1988) had a long career, from 1944 to 1983, with Burroughs Wellcome, a pharmaceutical company based in North Carolina.

EXHIBIT V
UNIVERSITY AFFILIATIONS

Jewish Nobel Laureates in Science and Medicine
Columbia and Harvard Universities

* In chronological order

Laureates Prize / Year	B.S. / B.A. M.S.	Ph.D. or M.D.	Faculty/ Other
Rabi, Isidor Physics 1944	Cornell	**Columbia**	**Columbia**
Muller, Hermann Medicine 1946	**Columbia** **Columbia**	**Columbia**	**Columbia** **U. Texas/Austin** **U. Indiana**
Lipmann, Fritz Medicine 1953	Königsberg (Germany)	Berlin (Germany)	Rockefeller **Harvard**
Lederberg, Joshua Medicine 1958	**Columbia**	**Columbia**	Rockefeller Stanford U. Wisconsin
Bloch, Konrad Medicine 1964	Munich (Germany)	**Columbia**	**Harvard** **Columbia** Chicago
Schwinger, Julian Physics 1965	C.C.N.Y.	**Columbia**	U.C.L.A **Harvard**
Wald, George Medicine 1967	N.Y.U. **Columbia**	**Columbia**	**Harvard**
Luria, Salvador Medicine 1969	Torino (Italy) **Columbia**	Torino (Italy)	M.I.T. Chicago U. Indiana

Laureates Prize / Year	B.S. / B.A. M.S.	Ph.D. or M.D.	Faculty/ Other
Cooper, Leon Physics 1972	**Columbia** **Columbia**	**Columbia**	Brown
Stein, William Chemistry 1972	**Harvard** **Columbia**	**Columbia**	Rockefeller
Mottelson, Benjamin Physics 1975	Purdue	**Harvard**	Copenhagen (Denmark)
Blumberg, Baruch Medicine 1976	Union	**Columbia** Oxford (England)	U. Pennsylvania Oxford (England) NASA
Penzias, Arno Physics 1978	C.C.N.Y. **Columbia**	**Columbia**	Bell Labs Princeton
Nathans, Daniel Medicine, 1978	U. Delaware **Columbia**	Washington U. of St. Louis	Johns Hopkins
Glashow, Sheldon Physics 1979	Cornell **Harvard**	**Harvard**	**Harvard** U. Cal./Berkeley
Weinberg, Steven Physics 1979	Cornell	Princeton	U. Texas/Austin **Harvard** U. Cal./Berkeley
Benacerraf, Baruj Medicine 1980	**Columbia** **Columbia**	Medical College of Virginia	**Harvard** N.Y.U.
Gilbert, Walter Chemistry 1980	**Harvard** **Harvard**	Cambridge (England)	**Harvard**
Hoffmann, Roald Chemistry 1981	**Columbia** **Harvard**	**Harvard**	Cornell
Schawlow, Arthur Physics 1981	Toronto (Canada) **Columbia**	**Toronto** **(Canada)**	Stanford Bell Labs **Columbia**

Laureates Prize / Year	B.S. / B.A. M.S.	Ph.D. or M.D.	Faculty/ Other
Hauptman, Herbert Chemistry 1985	C.C.N.Y. **Columbia**	U. Maryland	U.S. Naval Research Lab U. Buffalo
Karle, Jerome Chemistry 1985	C.C.N.Y. **Harvard**	U. Michigan	U.S. Naval Research Lab U. Maryland
Lederman, Leon Physics 1988	C.C.N.Y. **Columbia**	**Columbia**	Illinois Tech. Fermi Lab **Columbia**
Schwartz, Melvin Physics 1988	**Columbia**	**Columbia**	**Columbia** Stanford Bell Labs
Steinberger, Jack Physics 1988	Chicago	Chicago	**Columbia**
Varmus, Harold Medicine 1989	Amherst **Harvard**	**Columbia**	National Inst. Health U. Cal./ San Francisco
Perl, Martin Physics 1995	New York Polytechnic	**Columbia**	Stanford U. Michigan
Lee, David Physics 1996	**Harvard**	Yale	Texas A&M Cornell
Kohn, Walter Chemistry 1990	Toronto (Canada)	**Harvard**	U. Cal./Santa Barbara U. Cal./San Diego Carnegie-Mellon
Kandel, Eric Medicine 2000	**Harvard**	N.Y.U.	**Columbia** N.Y.U.
Horvitz, H. Robert Medicine 2002	M.I.T. **Harvard**	**Harvard**	M.I.T.

Laureates Prize / Year	B.S. / B.A. M.S.	Ph.D. or M.D.	Faculty/ Other
Axel, Richard Medicine 2004	**Columbia**	Johns Hopkins	**Columbia**
Politzer, David Physics 2004	U. Michigan	**Harvard**	Cal. Tech
Glauber, Roy Physics 2005	**Harvard**	**Harvard**	**Harvard**
Kornberg, Roger Chemistry 2006	**Harvard**	Stanford	Stanford Hebrew U. (Israel)
Chalfie, Martin Chemistry 2008	**Harvard**	**Harvard**	Columbia
Perlmutter, Saul Physics 2011	**Harvard**	U. Cal./Berkeley	U. Cal./Berkeley
Riess, Adam Physics 2011	M.I.T.	**Harvard**	Johns Hopkins
Steinman, Ralph Medicine 2011	McGill (Canada)	**Harvard**	Rockefeller
Lefkowitz, Robert Chemistry 2012	**Columbia**	**Columbia**	Duke
Rothman, James Medicine 2013	Yale	**Harvard**	Yale **Columbia**
Karplus, Martin Chemistry 2013	**Harvard**	Cal. Tech	**Harvard** **Columbia**
Ashkin, Arthur Physics, 2018	**Columbia**	Cornell	Bell Labs

X. From Barriers to Breakthroughs: The Jewish American Experience

Typical of his times, President Lawrence Lowell of Harvard in 1922 recommended imposing a 15% admissions quota (*numerus clausus*) on Jewish students (10% at Yale, and only 3% at Princeton). "Unless the number of Jews at Harvard were reduced," he explained, "antisemitism would only become stronger in American education." His byzantine logic: "If every college in the country would take a limited proportion of Jews...we should go a long way toward eliminating race-feelings among students, and as these students passed out into the world, eliminate it in the country."[31] Meanwhile at Yale, Dean Frederick Jones noted that, "Any single scholarship of any value was won by a Jew, and we could not let that go on. We must put a ban on Jews." Henceforth admissions should be based on character since, "In terms of scholarship and intelligence, Jewish students lead the class, but their personal characteristics make them markedly inferior."[32]

As late as 1948, the U.S. President's Commission on Higher Education reported that Jewish students did not have equal opportunity for admission to colleges because of the quota systems.

---

31 Sachar, Howard M. *A History of the Jews in America*. New York: Knopf, 1992, p. 329

32 Hertzberg, Arthur. *The Jews in America: Four Centuries of an Uneasy Encounter: A History*. New York: Simon and Schuster, 1989, p. 234

When the admission restrictions were lifted, the number of Jews attending college and professional schools, especially Ivy League and other elite universities, swelled. President Lowell would have been shocked to learn that by the 1950s as much as thirty percent of the student body of Harvard College was Jewish, though not fully reflected in college records. At the time the admission questionnaire asked for religious affiliations. Many of the students answering "none" or agnostic, or who left the space blank were likely to be Jewish, based on their last names and biographical data.

How things have changed. In 2002 *The Wall Street Journal* featured a front-page article, "Colleges Court Jewish Students in Effort to Boost Rankings." It reported that Vanderbilt University in Nashville, Tennessee, was seeking to enroll Jewish students to raise its academic standing. Despite their religious denominations, Southern Methodist University and Texas Christian University were also pursuing Jewish students. Like Vanderbilt, SMU acknowledged the academic aspirations underlying these overtures: "There appears to be a strong correlation between the quality of your student body and the size of your Jewish population."[33]

Medical discoveries and innovations have been particularly beneficial to human well-being. Worldwide, Jews have obtained 26% of all medicine awards while American Jews have been awarded 41% of all U.S. prizes for medicine. The proverbial Jewish parents' refrain, "our son, the doctor" or "our daughter married a doctor" reflects medicine's deep-seated prestige. The Jewish tradition in medicine goes back a long way. It flourished for centuries in pre-Inquisition Spain. During many centuries when

---

33 "Colleges Court Jewish Students in Effort to Boost Rankings." *The Wall Street Journal* 29 April 2002

Jews were confined to ghettos—and in spite of papal orders forbidding Christians to be treated by Jews—the rich and powerful, including kings and even popes, sought Jewish physicians. The breakthrough for Jews began in the nineteenth century when Jews were admitted to medical schools in Central and Western Europe.

For those seeking a medical career in the U.S. in earlier years of the 20th century, admission to medical schools was even more difficult than admission to college. The quotas in the medical schools forced many young Jews to go to Europe for their medical education. Even after when they were accepted, there still were problems. Fifty years after its occurrence, Emory University in 2012 publicly apologized for years of discrimination at its dental school. Symptomatic of the times, Jewish students were sometimes flunked or forced to repeat courses because of Anti-Semitism.[34] After they graduated, Jewish doctors were still in trouble. The Gentile-controlled hospitals allowed very few Jews to join their staffs. Jewish sponsored hospitals existed not so much to take care of Jewish patients as to provide places in which Jewish doctors could practice. At the same time few Jewish professors could obtain appointments on the faculties of American medical schools.

While medicine was the category with the largest number of American Jewish Nobel laureates, chemistry had the fewest, with 27% of U.S. honorands (versus 41% in medicine and 40% in physics). Six European Jews had already been chemistry prizewinners in the first six decades of the Nobel Prize, but it was not until 1961 that an American Jew, Melvin Calvin, received the chemistry

---

34 Lieber, Chavie. "Atlanta's Emory apologizes for anti-Semitism." *Miami Herald,* Oct. 2012

Dr. Melvin Calvin, Director of the Chemical Biodynamics Laboratory at Lawrence Berkeley Laboratory, works in his photosynthesis laboratory.

award. By way of contrast, more than a half century earlier Albert Michelson received the physics award in 1907. It may not be accidental that chemistry is the field of science with the fewest Jewish Nobel laureates. "On the eve of WWII institutional Anti-Semitism remained a barrier in American science, and a higher barrier for graduate schools than colleges...industrial companies that conducted most research in applied sciences were largely closed to Jews." In 1946, Albert Coolidge, Chairman of Harvard's Chemistry Department, explained, "We know perfectly well that names ending in 'berg' or 'stein' have to be skipped...because there are no jobs for Jews in chemistry."[35]

---

35 Gleick, James. *Genius: The Life and Science of Richard Feynman.* New York: Pantheon, 1992, pp. 84–85

The barriers confronting those who wanted teaching careers in universities were even greater than those affecting students' enrollment. Until well after World War II, there were relatively few Jewish faculty members, especially in leading universities and professional schools. George Birkhoff, a Harvard professor who ran the mathematics department with an iron hand from 1912 to 1944, was able to keep Harvard from hiring any Jewish mathematicians—even the renown John von Neumann. Birkhoff's role was revealed in a book published by the Harvard University Press in 2013.[36] His ability to sway Harvard for so long was at least partially due to the latent antisemitism, not unlike what prevailed at the time in most universities.

In 1945 Ernest Hopkins, then President of Dartmouth College, justified their tight Jewish quota by explaining, "Dartmouth is a Christian college, founded for the Christianization of its students."[37] Only decades later, it was a whole different story. Jewish professors abounded in the faculty of America's leading universities, medical and law schools. Not only that, but Jews came to head up numerous of these institutions. How ironic that by 1970, just twenty-five years after Hopkins' comment, John Kemeny, who was Jewish, was named president of Dartmouth, and six years after his retirement in 1987, another Jew, James Freedman, was named president.

Former Dartmouth President John Kemeny

---

36 Nadis, Steven J., and Shing-Tung Yau. *A History in Sum: 150 Years of Mathematics at Harvard (1825–1975)*. Cambridge, MA: Harvard University Press, 2013.

37 Ibid, Sacher, p.753

Nowadays naming a Jewish president of a university is not news-worthy. Many of the most prestigious universities in the United States have, or have had Jewish presidents, to name a few: Harvard (Lawrence Summer, Lawrence Bacow), Yale (Richard Levin), M.I.T. (Jerome Weisner, Rafael Reif), Princeton (Harold Shapiro) Columbia (Michael Sovern), University of Chicago (Edwin Levi), Cornell (Jeffrey Lehman), and the University of Pennsylvania (Judith Rodin, Amy Gutmann).

Harvard President Lawrence Bacow, 2018

Having overcome discrimination and restrictions in higher education, American Jews flourished not only in science and academia, but also in the professions, especially medicine and law, in which Jews are greatly over-represented. In the business world, Jews traditionally have been most successful when they created their own businesses and did not depend on others for employment. Entrepreneurial American Jews' early prominence in the world of finance/investments,[38] retailing, and the motion picture industry is legendary.[39]

Employment in major U.S. industrial corporations, however, was another matter. Until the 1950s Jews faced serious hiring and promotion barriers. Few industrialists were as notoriously antisemitic as Henry Ford. However, in many of the largest U.S.

38 Birmingham, Stephen. *Our Crowd: The Great Jewish Families of New York*. New York: Harper & Row, 1967. Ehrlich, Judith Ramsey, and Barry J. Rehfeld. *The New Crowd: The Changing of the Jewish Guard On Wall Street*. Boston: Little, Brown, 1989.

39 Gabler, Neal. *An Empire of their Own: How the Jews Invented Hollywood*. New York: Crown Publishers, 1988.

corporations, even entry level positions were difficult for qualified young Jewish graduates to obtain. One of the earliest, high visibility breakthroughs involved one of the oldest and most prestigious American companies—DuPont. Once among the most impenetrable companies for Jewish executives, DuPont appointed Irving Shapiro C.E.O. and Chairman of the Board in 1974. Such designations now have become so commonplace that they are hardly noted. By and large Jews can rise to the top echelons of the corporate ladder.

With achievement and success there has also been giving back in a material way. Jewish donors are consistently over-represented in the annual listing of most generous philanthropists. In *Forbes* magazine 2019 list of 50 top donors, 20 (40%) were Jewish. Overall, not just the very wealthy, American Jews donate more to charities and public causes than Americans in general of comparable income level. Their philanthropy is not limited to Jewish and Israeli causes, but also extends to education, health, medical research, and the arts.

XI. Why the Exceptionalism?

"I will insist that the Hebrews have done more to civilize men than any other nation. If I were an atheist and believed in blind eternal fate, I should still believe that fate had ordained the Jews to be the most essential instrument for civilizing the nations...They are the most glorious nation that ever inhabited this earth. The Romans and their empire were but a bauble in comparison of the Jews. They have given religion to three-quarters of the globe and have influenced the affairs of mankind more and more happily than any other nation, ancient or modern."

—JOHN ADAMS, second President of the United States,
from a letter to F.A. Van Der Kamp, 1808 (National Archives)

"Some people like the Jews, and some do not. But no thoughtful man can deny the fact that they are, beyond any question, the most formidable and most remarkable race which has appeared in the world."

—WINSTON CHURCHILL, *Illustrated Sunday Herald,*
Feb. 8, 1920

Why are Jews so over-represented among Nobel science prize-winners? What accounts for their outsized achievements and contributions in so many fields of human endeavor? Jewish cultural values based on family upbringing, dedication to education, self-motivation, persistence, resilience in face of adversity, and just plain hard work undoubtedly contribute to their success.

Traditionally the Jewish family has been a stable and nurturing unit. The incidences of family violence, abandonment, failure to provide support for wife and children, alcoholism, unwed mothers, and other social ills are relatively rare. Thomas Sowell, a noted black sociologist, commented in his book *Ethnic America: A History*, "Despite the voluminous literature claiming that the slums shape people's values, the Jews had their own values...Even when Jews lived in the slums, they were slums with a difference—lower alcoholism, homicide, and accidental death rates than other slums, or even the city as a whole. Their children had lower truancy rates, lower juvenile delinquency rates, and higher IQs than other children."[40]

Family size also matters. Overall, Jewish families in modern times have considerably fewer children than the average birthrate. Consequently, Jewish parents have been able to dedicate more time and money to each child's welfare, education and cultural development.

Above all, Jewish families have always placed great emphasis on education. Jews have a long history of dedication to learning going back to ancient times. Judaism required every Jewish man to study the Torah and the Talmud, which necessitated literacy. This was in marked contrast to Christianity, which, until the end of the medieval times, left literacy largely to the clergy. "At a time when

---

40 Sowell, Thomas. *Ethnic America: A History*. New York: Basic Books, 1981, p. 98.

nearly all Christian and Muslim men, and certainly women, were illiterate, nearly all Jewish men and women could read and write, and many of them achieved high levels of knowledge." The great Catholic theologian Abelard reported, "A Jew however poor, if he had ten sons would put them all to letters, not for gain, as Christians do, but for the understanding of God's law, and not only his sons but his daughters."[41]

Roger Kornberg (Chemistry 2006) and his father, Arthur Kornberg (Medicine 1959), father and son Nobel prizewinners.

Jews valued learning for itself as well as a means of making progress. Again and again the Jewish Nobel prizewinners in science relate how their parents encouraged their love for learning. It is not uncommon to have these parents—even those with minimal education themselves—prioritize education for their children.

---

41 Dennis Prager and Joseph Telushkin, *Why the Jews?* New York: Simon & Schuster, 1983, p.48.

Whereas most parents in poor or modest circumstances are anxious for their offspring to join the workforce, Jewish parents, including the poor, have been willing to make sacrifices so that their children could remain in school as long as possible. This deep-seated belief in the value of education is evident whether the family is observant or non-religious. Once education became readily accessible, Jews, with their long tradition of valuing learning, were in an excellent position to take full advantage of the opportunities when they presented themselves.

The Jewish psyche may embody feelings of both inferiority and superiority simultaneously. It is not surprising that Jewish children who have been bullied or have been the object of discrimination because they were "different" could develop feelings of inferiority. At home, however, Jewish children are brought up to have high esteem for their families, their people, and themselves. Self-esteem breeds a belief in one's worth and ability, no matter what negative views prevail in the outside world.

The drive to excel and not to be satisfied with average results are important traits often instilled in young Jews. Children of immigrant parents especially felt the need to succeed to recompense their parents for their sacrifices. Beyond the first generation, parents continued to instill high expectations in their in their offspring ("You got a B+, so what's wrong with an A?"). In time, these expectations became inculcated, as well a sense of obligation, reinforced perhaps by the proverbial "Jewish guilt." Shimon Peres, one of Israel's founders and a prime minister, once remarked, "There is something in our DNA that makes us Jews never feel satisfied."[42]

---

42 *The Weapon Wizards: How Israel Became a High-Tech Military Superpower,* Yaakov Katz & Amir Bohbot, St. Martin's Press, N.Y., 2017, p. 266

Jews have frequently succeeded when others have given up the struggle in spite of facing restrictions on where they could live (the ghettos), with whom they could associate, and which trades they could practice. Persecution, physical abuse, and even annihilation, in some ways may actually have strengthened Jews' resolve and tenacity. Resilience is a defining characteristic of the Jewish people, as their very survival through their long and painful history attests.

In many countries Jews often felt like outsiders, not fully accepted by their countrymen. This "otherness" may have given them a further incentive to strive to prove their worth rather than complacently accept their lot in life. Often differing from the general culture, Jews have been less likely to cling to conventional wisdom and preconceptions. That allowed them to be more open to change, to adapt more quickly to new circumstances, and to perceive new opportunities.

Historically, Jews have often been negatively characterized as greedy and unscrupulous. The figure of the Jewish money lender (one of the few trades open to Jews for hundreds of years) was an antisemitic stereotype for centuries. The accumulation of wealth for a better life has always been a motivating factor and the most measurable reward of success. For Jews, with a history of persecutions and expulsions, financial resources could mean even more—a lifesaver in desperate situations.

The foregoing cultural and historical factors shed some light on the reasons for Jewish achievement, but some authorities on the subject have pointed out other factors to consider. Ernest Van Den Haag, an influential psychoanalyst and former professor at New York University, wrote: "In a world where Jews are only a tiny percentage of the population, what is the secret of the disproportionate importance the Jews have had in the history of Western culture? Are they, as both their friends and enemies seem to suspect, smarter than other people? The I.Q. test is far from a perfect measure. Still, when we find that genetically identical twins reared in different environments have nearly identical scores, while brothers and sisters reared in the same environment display greater IQ differences, the conclusion that inheritance plays a major role is inescapable. And the average IQs of Jewish children are consistently higher than those of non-Jewish children."[43]

Three Identical Strangers, the 2018 documentary film, chronicled the astonishing case of identical triplets separated at birth. They were adopted by different families who were not made aware of the existence of other siblings. The undisclosed separations were part of a clinical study of the effects on identical siblings (mostly twins) when they were brought up in different environments. It turned out that the subjects were incredibly similar in spite of the very dissimilar socioeconomic status of the households in which they were placed. It is doubtful that this kind of study will ever be repeated as the study's revelation caused public outcry. Though the results are not statistically significant because of the small base, the findings nevertheless are indicative the strong role of inheritance.

Harvard psychologists Richard Herrnstein and Charles Murray documented the relationship between IQ and achievement in their massive work *The Bell Curve.* They also raised the question, "Are Jews really smarter than anyone else?" Their conclusion: "Jews—specifically Ashkenazi Jews of European origins—test higher than any other ethnic group.... These test results are matched by

---

43 Van Den Haag, Ernest. *The Jewish Mystique* New York: Stein & Day, 1969, pp. 13–14

analyses of occupational and scientific attainment by Jews, which consistently show their disproportionate level of success, usually by orders of magnitude, in various inventories of scientific and artistic achievement."[44]

In the College Board's rare ranking of SAT college admissions scores by religion, Unitarian/Universalists placed first, then Jews, Quakers, and Hindus.[45] Results on tests like the IQ and college boards should not simplistically be equated to intelligence. There are different aspects of intelligence that cannot be measured by testing. Furthermore, these tests may contain inherent cultural biases that could affect the results. Besides, some individuals just are not good at taking tests. It is obvious that intelligence by itself does not lead to achievement. High IQ without motivation and perseverance is unlikely to result in significant accomplishments.

Historical and cultural factors do not appear to fully account for the phenomenon of Jewish achievement. It would appear that some inherited influence is present, realizing that nurture and nature are inextricably intertwined. It will have to be left to the scientific community to unravel the mystery of genetic influence in human beings. Until then, the polemic goes on.

Jews certainly do not have a monopoly on exceptionalism. Jewish immigrants from Russia and Eastern Europe admitted to the United States around the turn of the twentieth century were largely uneducated and considered to have subpar intelligence. Yet their offspring were able to ascend to high levels of achievement in one or two generations. Over time, some groups will come to

---

44 Richard Herrnstein and Richard Murray, *The Bell Curve* New York: The Free Press, 1994, p. 275

45 Front page, *The Wall Street Journal*, April 29, 2002

the forefront, while others fade away. Witness the disappearance of the Roman Empire, the dissolution of the British Empire and the recent rise of China as a world power. The only certainty is that things are bound to change. Change is not only possible, it is inevitable.

XII. The Outlook

"May the children of the stock of Abraham who dwell in this land continue to merit and enjoy the goodwill of the other inhabitants."

—From a plaque in the Touro Synagogue, Newport, Rhode Island, based on a 1789 letter from George Washington to the Hebrew Congregation of Newport

America has been good to the Jews, and the Jews have been good for America. It has fulfilled the immigrants' hopes for a better life, even though that may have come to pass in a later generation. At the same time, the U.S. has greatly benefited from the multiple talents of its citizens of Jewish origin.

The outlook is for the United States to remain the dominant force in scientific achievement, including Nobel science prizes. Besides its native-born talent, top scientists from abroad will continue to come to the United States, attracted by the country's technological and educational infrastructure, better funding resources, and higher remuneration. Throughout this book it has been evident that a close relationship exists between the scientific achievements of this nation and its Jewish citizens.

Can Jews keep up their record of achievement? In the long run, probably not; at least not to the same extent as in the past or at present. The modern low Jewish birthrate has not kept pace with population growth, becoming an ever-decreasing percentage of the population of the United States as well as the rest of the world. In the U.S., the percentage of the population that is Jewish has shrunk from 3.5% in 1930 to 2% presently.

The situation is even more precarious worldwide. From estimates of a high of 17 million in 1939 to some 15 million in 2016, the Jewish population has declined since then, while the world's population has burgeoned. The six million Jews killed in the Holocaust corresponded to 36% of all Jews in the world at that time. In U.S. terms this would have equaled the deaths of some fifty million Americans at that time. Demographically speaking, Jews still have not recovered from the losses of the Holocaust. If it were not for Orthodox Jews, who rarely marry outside the faith and have a high birthrate, the numbers would be even lower.

From a purely demographic perspective, assimilation rather than discrimination has been a problem. Having gradually shed some of their Jewish values and lifestyles, American Jews have become so well integrated that they often are hardly distinguishable from the mainstream. American society, at the same time, has become more diverse. The final measure of assimilation and social acceptance is inter-marriage. Until the 1960s, marriage between Jews and Christians was fairly uncommon. Since then it has accelerated until it has become commonplace; so common that American Jews are now as likely to marry a Christian spouse as they are to marry a co-religionist.

In mixed marriages, the children are more likely to identify with the Christian partner, especially when it is the mother. Others are brought up non-religiously. Even those children raised Jewish in mixed marriages are likely to have a weaker Jewish identity. They are more likely to marry a non-Jewish spouse and, within another generation or two, their Jewish heritage is likely to have faded away completely. Integration into American society while desirable, may also result in diminishing the Jewish cultural values that have propelled achievement in the past.

While some of the earlier Jewish immigrant generations' fervor to succeed may have weakened, Chinese, Indian, and other Asians immigrants are exhibiting many behavioral patterns similar to the Jews. These Asians also share cultural values, such as family stability, emphasis on education, sense of obligation, willingness to postpone gratification, tenacity, and dedication to hard work. Their children excel in the halls of academia and are making strong in-roads in science and the professions.

Asian Americans have already made significant contributions to science and are likely to play an even more important role in the near future. Furthermore, the large number of Asians studying and working in the United States and Western countries will augment the globalization of science. On the home front several Asian countries are gearing up their own technological infrastructure. These developments are likely to significantly increase the role of Asians in scientific achievements and consequently lead to a more prominent presence among Nobel Prize science prizewinners. Asians could also be affected by over-emphasis on affirmative action.

Quotas were originally set to curb the number of minorities (such as the *numerus clausus* limiting Jewish students), whereas affirmative action now tends to favor certain groups. Affirmative action has a role in fostering diversity as long as it is handled judiciously. Problems, however, may arise with the mindset that student bodies and organizations should reflect the percentage of the general population based on race, ethnicity, and gender. This would unfairly limit the opportunities and access of more qualified persons—whether they be members of a minority or majority group—which would be discriminatory to the individual. Beyond concern for the individual, the mindset of proportionality could be a hindrance to America's economic and technological leadership. There has to be a delicate balance between social goals and the rights of individuals affected.

The Jewish population of Europe, which provided so much talent before the Holocaust, is now but a shadow of itself. However, there is a worthy newcomer, Israel, which promises at least partially to fill the void left by its European counterparts' former scientific achievement. The country has become a world-class scientific and technological powerhouse. Israel's formidable achievements and contributions are documented in an appendix (see page 127).

As for Nobel prizes, Israelis are coming into their own having won six Nobel science awards since 2001 (as well as six additional awards in non-scientific fields). This is a good beginning for a country that is little more than seventy years in existence considering the average age of Nobel Prize science award winners is around sixty years. Israel already ranks eleventh

Arieh Warshel, Chemistry Laureate 2013

among the top nations in science laureates on a per capita basis. Symptomatically a brain drain has already started as Israeli scientists move to the United States where there is less competition and better pay and funding. Arieh Warshel[C] (Chemistry 2013) left Israel for the U.S. because he couldn't find an appropriate position. He asserted that Israel has too many bright scientists and too few available jobs. Israeli scientists are likely to partially replace the loss of European Jewish scientists' contribution as a result of the Holocaust.

Returning to the original query: Can Jews keep up their record of achievement? In the long run, the number of Jewish science Nobel prizewinners is likely to decrease in total number for the reasons previously cited. The disproportionate aspect, however, will probably continue. In the near future (there is a time lag), Jewish *uber* achievement is likely to continue if recent trends are any indication. For the first fifty years (1901–1950) of the Nobel Prize there were only 28 Jewish prizewinners in medicine, physics and chemistry, likely due to the prevailing antisemitism. By comparison, just from 2000 to 2018, there were 35 Jewish honorands (27 of whom were born in the U.S.), almost a fourfold increase taking into consideration the number of years. 2013 was a banner year with six of the eight Nobel science prizes awarded to Jewish scientists, five of them Americans.

In conclusion, what conditions are necessary to broaden the scope of scientific achievement? Education, no doubt, is fundamental. Without the proper educational infrastructure, scientific pursuit is stunted at the outset. Scientific activities flourish with the support of a society that values and rewards critical thinking and innovation. The lack of these conditions goes a long way toward explaining why so few world-class scientists have emerged from developing countries. Those few who have reached that level studied or worked in developed countries. It is one thing to grow up in Ouagadougou, another in Frankfurt.

In one such effort to stimulate the globalization of science, the Lindau Institute, based in Bavaria, Germany, holds annual meetings, bringing together Nobel science prizewinners and outstanding science students from around the world "to foster successful exchange between different generations and cultures." Typically, in 2019, more than thirty science laureates are expected with some 600 promising young scientists from 48 nations. Outreach continues after these meetings.

Though not usually mentioned as a factor, climate also can be a significant element in accounting for scientific achievement. Empirically there appears to be a close relationship between climate and a nation's standard of living, level of progress, and innovation. Whatever their nationality, ethnicity or religion outstanding scientists have overwhelmingly been born, educated and made their discoveries in countries with temperate climates. Year-long heat not only saps energy but also affects mental acuity. The broader use of air conditioning should help bring about more scientific activity in warmer climates.

These socioeconomic considerations may be necessary for progress in science and human development, but it is an individual's intelligence and drive that creates an outstanding scientist. Intellect is a prerequisite, but it also takes a unique combination of personal qualities to propel one to the highest levels of scientific achievement. These include such traits as an inquisitive mind, innovative thinking, intense motivation, persistence, and hard work. Passion and dedication are necessary in the pursuit of one's goals, which often means sacrificing family involvement and forgoing other interests. Whatever their background, individuals who have these highly developed attributes, "the right stuff," can aspire to be scientific achievers and contribute to knowledge and human welfare.

APPENDIX

Israel:
Inventions and Innovations

Israel is, by many measures, the country,
relative to its population, that's done the most to
contribute to the technology revolution.[46]

—BILL GATES

A country founded against all odds, Israel not only has survived, but has thrived. Although it has been a nation only
since 1948, Israel is home to world-class scientific educational
institutions such as the Weizmann Institute (Tel Aviv), the Technion (Haifa), and Hebrew University (Jerusalem). It has the
world's highest spending per capita on research and development,
as well as the highest number per capita of university graduates in
medicine, science, and engineering. Israel has become a scientific
and technological powerhouse with high tech and biotech start-up
companies exceeded in total only by the United States and China.
The Israeli government encourages technological progress by providing venture capital and tax breaks for start-ups.

Israel's prowess in inventions and innovations—electronics, com-
puter software, cyber-technology, defense systems, pharmaceuti-
cals and medical devices—is well known and has been adopted
worldwide. To highlight some recent ones: The emergency

---

46. untoldnews@tinydynamobook.com

bandage (also called "Israel bandage") that can stop hemorrhagic bleeding from traumatic injuries in emergency situations; the "PillCam"—an ingested endoscopic pill-sized camera that can diagnose digestive tract disorders; "Rewalk"—a bionic robotic device that helps patients with spinal cord injuries to stand up and walk; "Orcam"—a tiny smart camera that assists the visually impaired by reading texts audibly; "Mobileye"—which enables self-drive vehicles to detect road hazards to avoid accidents; and the "Waze" navigation app. It's no wonder that major U.S. companies—Intel, Google, IBM, Apple, Microsoft, and Cisco—have established R&D facilities and joint ventures in Israel or bought startup companies outright to tap into local talent. As a young entrepreneur in Be'er-Sheva at the new Negev Desert research complex explained, "Israel's main export is brains."

Denied arms to protect itself from its hostile neighbors at its inception, Israel had to create weapons and defense systems industries from scratch. The country is a world leader in military technology such as satellites, drones, missile defense systems and cyber warfare. Constant inventiveness has been required to maintain its leadership and keep one step ahead. Israel has revolutionized satellite information gathering capabilities. It developed the "Iron Dome" missile defense program to intercept enemy missiles, a constant threat on its borders.

The Israel Defense Forces have been instrumental in shaping Israeli life and leadership in technology. Soldiers are trained in mathematics and physics while serving in the military. After their compulsory three-year service, many are employed in industry to take advantage of what they learned in the military. The IDF has served as a breeding ground for new technology, generating spin-off firms that have bolstered Israel's hi-tech exports. As stated by

Shimon Peres, "To retain Israel's qualitative edge we need to invest in soldiers' brains, not just their muscles."[47]

Israel's contributions have not been limited to the military. This tiny country, with few natural resources and little arable land, had to have ingenuity not only to survive, but also to prosper. It has turned empty, dusty land into highly productive agricultural fields. The country's greenery is in stark contrast to the barren lands beyond its borders. Israel is at the forefront of water technology, providing solutions to acute water supply problems. It has become a major supplier of desalinization plants and a leader in the use of sea water to provide agricultural and drinking water. It even exports water to neighboring Jordan and Egypt. Israel developed the drip irrigation system that not only saves water, but also increases crop quantity and quality. It is the world leader in recycling water, reusing 86% of its treated waste water for irrigation. Israel has shared its knowledge and experience in this field, benefitting many nations around the world.

Forestation is another area of notable accomplishment. Since its earliest days Israel has planted 260 million trees to enhance its ecological environment. This concern is reflected in the tradition of planting a tree, a customary practice as many visitors to Israel are aware. Even in the Negev, the desert that makes up half of Israel's territory, acacia trees are being planted that can survive the extreme dry conditions. The country has uniquely succeeded in turning back the desert's encroachment to create more arable land.

Like their European forbearers, Israelis exhibit many traditional Jewish values, especially their devotion to the value of education.

47 *The Weapon Wizards: How Israel Became a High-Tech Military Superpower,* Yaakov Katz & Amir Bohbot, St. Martin's Press, N.Y., 2017, p. 266

Geographical realities have shaped Israel's resilience and character. Under constant threat of annihilation, they have their own unique ethos best described as *chutzpah*. Chutzpah means gall, nerve, unrestrained boldness, and assertiveness. Negatively, it can also connote rudeness, effrontery, shameless audacity, and brashness. Israelis are not so hampered by hierarchy and traditional ways of doing things, and are given wide latitude to follow their own judgment. Questioning is not only accepted, but expected—even in the military. Unlike most military and corporate organizations, Israel is "not willing to sacrifice flexibility for discipline, initiative for organization, and innovation for predictability."[48] These personal attributes may provide some insights into Israel's success.

---

48 *Start-Up Nation,* Dan Senor, Saul Singer, Twelve/Hachette Book Group, NY, 2009, p 98

Selected Biographical Profiles of Jewish Nobel Prizewinners

The biographical profiles of some of the Jewish Nobel prize-winners in medicine and science that follow are listed alphabetically. The selection of the biographical profiles was made randomly and does not indicate any less merit of those not included. These biographical profiles of laureates are designed to provide the reader with some relevant information about their personal, educational and career backgrounds. As brief sketches, they are not meant to fully cover the fullness of the lives and contributions of the laureates. The reasons for their awards are based on Nobel prize citations (Exhibit III and the biographical profiles that follow).

An asterisk * indicates a biographical profile in this section. Uppercase superscripts—M for medicine, P for physics, or C for chemistry—indicate that there is additional information in Exhibits I, III, and IV.

Most of the laureates made other significant discoveries and innovations before and/or after receiving their awards. Apart from the Nobel Prize itself, all of the honorands received many other distinctions, such as honorary university degrees and scientific awards too numerous to mention herein. Hopefully the profiles will elicit further interest in learning more about the lives and discoveries of these Nobelists from autobiographies and biographies in print and on the internet.

ZHORES ALFEROV

Nobel Prize Physics 2000

Zhores Alferov, Physics 2000, with Russian
President, Vladimir Putin

Zhores Ivanovich Alferov was born in 1930 in Vitebsk, Byelo-russ, then part of the Soviet Union, to a Belarusian father, Ivan Karpovich Alferov, and a Jewish mother, Anna Vladimirovna, née Rosenblum.

In 1952 Alferov graduated from the Lenin Electrotechnical Institute in Leningrad. A year later he joined the Ioffe Physical-Technical Institute where he earned a doctorate in physics and mathematics. He spent his entire career at Ioffe (since 1991 known as The Russian Academy of Science). Starting as a researcher, he was successively promoted until becoming the Academy's Director in 1987.

In 2000 he received the Nobel Prize in Physics with H. Kroemer and J. Kilby "for developing semiconductor heterostructures used in high-speed and optoelectronics" which laid the foundation for the modern era of computers and information technology. The three scientists proposed the solid-state laser, which enabled today's fiber-optic communications and led to communication satellites, bar-code readers, and cellular telephones. An official of the Swedish Royal Academy of Sciences, which awards the Nobel Prizes, commented: "Without Alferov, it would not be possible to transfer all the information from satellites down to Earth or have so many telephone lines."[49]

Alferov was an influential member of the Duma, Russia's parliament. He advocated for state support of scientific research and opposed President Vladimir Putin's policy of religionization of Russia.

---

49 "Russian and Americans Share Hi-tech," *BBC News,* October 10, 2000

SIDNEY ALTMAN

Nobel Prize Chemistry 1989

Sydney Altman was born in Montreal, Canada, in 1939, to a poor immigrant family. His father was a grocer and his mother worked in a textile mill. Altman noted in his autobiography that he knew early in his life that "the path of opportunity was through education. No sacrifice was too great to forward our education and, fortunately, books and the tradition of study was not unknown in our family."[50]

He received his B.S. in physics at the Massachusetts Institute of Technology (MIT) in 1960. He recalls, "There I experienced four years of over-stimulation among brilliant, arrogant, and zany peers and outstanding teachers."[49] Altman went on to graduate studies at Columbia University and then to the University of Colorado where he earned a Ph.D. in 1967. He was invited to join the faculty of Yale University in 1971, was promoted to full professor in 1980, and became Chairman of the Department of Biology in 1983. He was Dean of Yale College from 1985 to 1990. Thereafter, he remained at Yale as a professor of molecular, cellular, and developmental biology and chemistry.

Altman and Thomas Cech were awarded the 1989 Nobel Prize in Chemistry, "for their discovery of catalytic properties of RNA." Their findings contributed to our understanding of how cells function, how genetic data transfers, and how to strengthen the body's defenses against viral attack.

---

50 "Sidney Altman—Biographical." Nobelprize.org

ARTHUR ASHKIN

Nobel Prize Physics 2018

Arthur Ashkin was born in 1922 in Brooklyn, the son of Isadore Ashkin, who ran a dental laboratory in Manhattan, and his wife Anna. His parents were Jewish immigrants from what used to be the Russian and Austro-Hungarian Empires, but are now in the Ukraine.

While attending Columbia University during World War II, Arthur Ashkin also worked as an enlisted Army reservist at Columbia Radiation Lab building magnetrons. He received a B.S. degree in physics from Columbia in 1947. He earned his Ph.D. in nuclear physics in 1952 at Cornell University, at the time also the academic home of physics Nobelists Hans Bethe (Physics 1967) and Richard Feynman (Physics 1965).

Ashkin joined Bell Labs in 1952, working first on microwaves and, later, on laser research. He conducted extensive research in experimental physics, developing 40 patents. He retired from Bell Labs after four decades. Ashkin felt that his work there, which formed the basis for the research that led to Steven Chen's 1997 Nobel Prize in physics, went unrecognized.

In 2018 Ashkin received the Nobel Prize in physics for "the invention of optical tweezers and their application to biological systems" that revolutionized laser eye surgery. According to The Royal

Swedish Academy of Sciences, "Ashkin showed how the radiation pressure of light could be harnessed to move physical objects without burning them, realising an old dream of science fiction."[51] He won half the monetary award; the other half was shared by Gérard Mourou (France) and Donna Strickland (Canada).

At ninety-six years old in 2018, Ashkin is the oldest person to ever win a Nobel Prize in any category. When he received the telephone call with the announcement that he had won the Nobel Prize in physics, he was still active at work on a new project in his home lab in Rumson, New Jersey.

---

51 *The Guardian,* Oct. 2, 2018

JULIUS AXELROD

Nobel Prize Medicine 1970

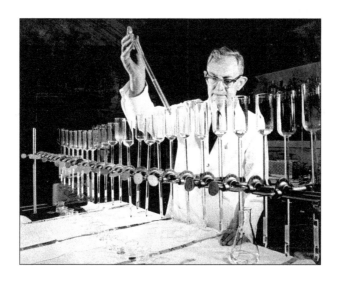

Julius Axelrod was born in 1912 on lower eastside of Manhattan to Isadore, a basket weaver, and his wife, Molly (nee Leichtling), Jewish immigrants from Poland. Brought up in a strict religious household, he rebelled at an early age becoming an atheist, although identifying with Jewish culture and causes. He obtained his B.S. degree from City College of New York and an M.A. from New York University. He applied to many medical schools, but was not admitted to any. Reflecting on these rejections, he told a newspaper reporter in 1970: "It was hard in those days for Jews to get into medical school. I wasn't that good a student, but if my name was Bigelow I probably would have gotten in."[52]

---

52 "The Julius Axelrod Papers." National Library of Medicine, *"Profiles in Science."*

While working as a technician at a laboratory at the New York City Department of Health he injured his left eye causing him to have to wear an eye patch for the rest of his life. Axelrod spent most of his career at the National Institutes of Health. Realizing that his advancement was limited without a Ph.D., he took a leave of absence to attend George Washington University Medical School, where he obtained a doctoral degree in 1955, returning afterward to the N.I.H.

Axelrod received the 1970 Nobel Prize in Medicine with co-honorands Bernard Katz[M] and Ulf von Euler for their work on the release and reuptake of catecholamine neurotransmitters. This laid the groundwork for brain chemical inhibitors such as Prozac. Earlier in his career, he discovered that replacing the previously used ingredient in analgesics with acetaminophen (better known as Tylenol) improved the product by eliminating side effects.

He died in 2004 in Rockville, Maryland, at the age of 92.

ADOLF VON BAEYER

Nobel Prize Chemistry 1905

Johann Friedrich Wilhelm Adolf von Baeyer was born in Berlin in 1835. He was the son of Johann Jakob Baeyer and Eugenie, née Hitzig, who was Jewish. His father, a general, came from a distinguished family in the arts and sciences.

Baeyer studied at the University of Heidelberg and received his doctorate in chemistry from the University of Berlin. His career was devoted to teaching and research at the University of Strassburg and later the University of Munich, where he was professor of chemistry.

Baeyer was the first person of partial Jewish origin to receive a Nobel Prize in science. He was the sole recipient of the Nobel Prize in Chemistry in 1905 "for the services he has rendered to the development of organic chemistry and the chemical industry through his work concerning organic dyes and hydrocarbon compounds." He declined to profit from the commercialization of his discoveries. On his 50th birthday he was granted the heredity title for his services to Germany, allowing him to add "von" to the family name noting nobility. He died at his country home in Starnberg See, Germany, in 1917.

ROBERT BARANY

Nobel Prize Medicine 1914

Robert Barany was born in Vienna, the capital of the Austro-Hungarian Empire, in 1876. His father, Ignaz, was a Hungarian bank official and his mother, Maria Hock, the daughter of a scientist. He received a medical degree from the University of Vienna in 1900.

He was the sole honorand of the Nobel Prize in Medicine in 1914 "for his work on the physiology and pathology of the vestibular apparatus" (inner ear). Barany's research demonstrated the important connections between the equilibrium apparatus and the central nervous system that are necessary to maintain the body's balance and coordination. He learned that he had won the Nobel Prize while serving in the medical corps of the Austro-Hungarian army during World War I. At the time he was imprisoned in Turkestan (then part of the U.S.S.R.). In spite of the intervention of Swedish royalty, two years passed before he could go to Stockholm to receive the award.

Barany left Vienna when he was accused of failing to acknowledge the contribution of his colleagues' research. Most of the charges were later shown to be unwarranted. He was invited to become principal of the Otological Institute of the University of Uppsala in Sweden where he remained until his death in 1936.

BARRY BARISH

Nobel Prize Physics 2017

Barry Barish was born in Omaha, Nebraska, in 1936, and raised in Los Angeles. His parents were Harold and Lee Barish, whose parents were immigrants from an area of Poland that is now part of Belarus.

Studying at the University of California at Berkeley, Barish earned his bachelors in physics in 1957 and his Ph.D. in experimental particle physics in 1962. Thereafter, he joined the California Institute of Technology (Caltech). He spent his entire academic career there, rising from a research fellow to an endowed chair in physics, and afterwards as Professor of Physics Emeritus.

Barish worked with the Laser Interferometer Gravitational-Wave Observatory (LIGO), which first detected the gravitational waves that Einstein had predicted more than a hundred years earlier. He succeeded Rainer Weiss* as its director. Barish was also significantly involved in a number of physics collaborations, from neutrino experiments at Fermilab to the Superconducting Collider.

He won the 2017 Nobel Prize in Physics with Rainer Weiss and Kip Thorne "for decisive contributions to the LIGO detector and the observation of gravitational waves." As Caltech president

Thomas Rosenbaum explained, "The first direct observation of gravitational waves by LIGO is an extraordinary demonstration of scientific vision and persistence. Through four decades of development of exquisitely sensitive instrumentation...we are now able to glimpse cosmic processes that were previously undetectable. It is truly the start of a new era in astrophysics."[53]

---

53 www.caltech.edu/content/2017-nobel-prize-physics

BARUJ BENACERRAF

Nobel Prize Medicine 1980

Baruj Benacerraf was born in Caracas, Venezuela, in 1920. His Sephardic Jewish parents were originally from Morocco and Algeria, which were French territories at the time. When he was five, they moved to Paris, where he completed his secondary education. The family returned to Venezuela in 1939 at the outbreak of the Second World War.

Benacerraf completed his pre-med requirements at Columbia University where he obtained a B.S. degree. Getting admitted into medical school was another matter. He attributed his numerous admission rejections to his ethnic and foreign background. He finally gained admission to the Medical College of Virginia through a friendly contact. Having become a naturalized U.S. citizen in 1943, he was drafted into the U.S. Army and commissioned as a First Lieutenant in the Medical Corps.

After completing post-graduate research at Columbia and in Paris, he joined New York University Medical School and, in 1956, was promoted to full professor. In 1970 he was appointed to the Chair of Pathology at Harvard Medical School.

Benacerraf was awarded the 1980 Nobel Prize in Medicine jointly with J. Dausset and G.D. Snell "for their discoveries concerning genetically determined structures on the cell surface that regulate immunological reactions."

He died in 2011 at the age of 91 in Boston, Massachusetts.

HANS BETHE

Nobel Prize Physics 1967

Hans Albrecht Bethe was born in 1906 in Strassburg, Germany, which is now Strasbourg, France. His Prussian Protestant father, Theodore Bethe, was a professor of medicine. His mother, née Anna Kuhn, was the daughter of a Jewish professor.

He obtained a Ph.D. in theoretical physics at the University of Munich in 1928. Shortly after starting with the University of Tubingen, he was dismissed when the Nazis came to power. Although he did not consider himself Jewish, he was nevertheless in jeopardy and immigrated to England in 1933.

In 1935 he moved to the U.S. and became a professor at Cornell University, where he remained for the rest of his professional career. The exception was the time he dedicated to the Manhattan Project during World War II. He was first assigned to the Radiation Laboratory at the Massachusetts Institute of Technology (M.I.T.) and later to Los Alamos Scientific Laboratory where he was engaged in a team assembling the first atomic bomb. In spite of his contributions to the atomic bomb and his work on the development of the hydrogen bomb, Bethe campaigned against nuclear testing and the nuclear arms race alongside other physicists.

Bethe was the sole honorand of the Nobel Prize in Physics in 1967 "for his contributions to the theory of nuclear reactions, especially his discoveries concerning the energy production in stars." Bethe's breadth of knowledge was extraordinarily extensive, covering many scientific fields.

He died in Ithaca, New York (home of Cornell), in 2005 at the age of 98.

BRUCE BEUTLER

Nobel Prize Medicine 2011

Bruce Alan Beutler, an immunologist and geneticist, was born in 1957 in Chicago, Illinois. His father, Ernest Beutler, was a professor and department chairman at The Scripps Research Institute in Southern California. His mother, Brondelle Fleisher, was a journalist. His parents had fled Berlin at the time of Hitler's takeover.

Beutler graduated from the University of California at San Diego at the age of 18. He went on to medical school at the University of Chicago and received his M.D. degree at age 23.

Starting in 1986, for the next fourteen years Beutler taught internal medicine at the University of Texas Southwestern Medical Center in Dallas. Following in his father's footsteps, in 2000 he accepted an appointment at The Scripps Research Institute as professor and chairman of the newly created Department of Genetics. In 2011, Beutler returned to U.T. Southwestern Medical Center as director of the Center for the Genetics of Host Defense.

He shared the honor of the 2011 Nobel Prize in Medicine with Jules Hoffman and Ralph Steinman[M] for "their discoveries concerning the activation of innate immunity." Their findings were used in developing drugs to treat inflammatory diseases.

FELIX BLOCH

Nobel Prize Physics 1952

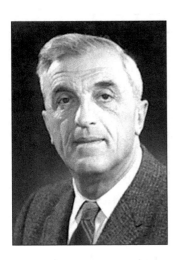

Felix Bloch was born in Zurich, Switzerland, in 1905 to Gustav and Agnes (nee Mayer) Bloch. He began his studies in physics at Zurich's Federal Institute of Technology and received his Ph.D. from the University of Leipzig (Germany) in 1928. Several research assignments thereafter gave him the opportunity to work with future Nobel prizewinners in physics, including Pauli,* Heisenberg, Bohr,* and Fermi.

With Hitler's ascent to power, Bloch left Germany in 1933 for a faculty appointment at Stanford University. Bloch became a U.S. citizen in 1939. During the Second World War, he was involved with the Manhattan Project, initially conducting nuclear power research at Los Alamos National Laboratory in New Mexico, and later working on a radar project at Harvard University. He returned to Stanford to teach physics and, in 1961, the university appointed him professor of an endowed chair.

He shared the 1952 Nobel Prize in Physics with Harvard physicist E.M. Purcell, who had reached the same conclusions independently. They were honored for their "development of new methods of nuclear magnetic precision measurement and discoveries in connection therewith."

Felix Bloch died in Zurich in 1983 at the age of 76.

KONRAD BLOCH

Nobel Prize Medicine 1964

German-American biochemist Konrad Emil Bloch was born in Neisse, Germany, now Nysa, Poland, in 1912, into a middle class family. He obtained the equivalent of an undergraduate degree in chemistry at the University of Munich in 1934. With the rise of the Nazi regime and the accompanying antisemitism, he sought refuge in Switzerland.

In 1936 Bloch was able to immigrate to the U.S. With the financial support of the Wallerstein Foundation, he enrolled in Columbia University's College of Physicians and Surgeons where he received his Ph.D. in biochemistry in 1938. After teaching at Columbia for six years, he received an appointment at the University of Chicago. In 1954 he moved to Harvard University to become chairman of the Department of Chemistry.

He shared the 1964 Nobel Prize in Medicine with Feodor Lynen "for their discoveries concerning the mechanisms and regulation of cholesterol and fatty acid metabolism," revealing how they are synthesized and metabolized in the body.

Konrad Bloch died in 2000 at the age of 88 in Burlington, Massachusetts.

BARUCH BLUMBERG

Nobel Prize Medicine 1976

Baruch "Barry" Samuel Blumberg was born in Brooklyn, New York, in 1925 to Meyer Blumberg, a lawyer, and his wife Ida, née Simonoff. He was brought up in a traditional religious Jewish family.

After completing active service in the Navy in 1943, he attended Union College in upstate New York where he received a B.S in physics. He enrolled in Columbia University's College of Physicians and Surgeons, obtaining his M.D. degree in 1951. He furthered his studies in England, earning a Ph.D. from Oxford University in 1957.

Blumberg had an unusually varied career including positions, sometimes simultaneously, with the National Institutes of Health, Fox Chase Cancer Center (Philadelphia), the University of Pennsylvania as professor of medicine, and Oxford as master of Balliol College. The latter named a professorship in urology in his honor. Throughout his career he traveled to some of the most remote parts of the world and lived among the natives to study infectious diseases.

He was awarded the Nobel Prize in Medicine in 1976 jointly with D.C. Gajdusek for "discoveries concerning new mechanisms for the origin and dissemination of infectious diseases." Blumberg is best known for the discovery of the antigen for hepatitis, derived from the blood of Australian aborigines, among whom he dwelled, as well as for the diagnostic test and vaccine for hepatitis.

Blumberg died in 2011 after giving a keynote speech at the NASA Lunar Science Institute in Mountain View, California, where he was a Distinguished Scientist.

NIELS BOHR

Nobel Prize Physics 1922

Niels Hendrik David Bohr was born in Copenhagen, Denmark, in 1885. He was the son of Christian Bohr, an eminent physiologist at the University of Copenhagen, and Ellen Bohr (nee Adler), daughter of a prominent Danish Jewish family. He obtained his bachelor's, master's, and doctorate degrees in physics (1911) from the University of Copenhagen.

In 1913, his alma mater offered him a physics professorship. Except for the World War II years, he remained associated with the University of Copenhagen his entire life. He headed up its Institute for Theoretical Physics (1920–1962), which was created especially for his research on the makeup of the atomic nuclei.

During the Nazi occupation of Denmark, Bohr was helped to escape by fishing boat to Sweden. He went on to England and then to the U.S. The Allies sought his expertise as a respected nuclear fission physicist, and invited him to join the Manhattan Project atomic bomb program in Los Alamos, New Mexico. Bohr met with President Franklin D. Roosevelt and Prime Minister Winston Churchill to express his deeply held concerns about atomic bomb proliferation.

He was the sole honorand of the 1922 Nobel Prize in Physics "for his services in the investigation of the structure of atoms and of the radiation emanating from them." In 1975, his son, Aage Bohr, also was awarded the Nobel Prize in Physics.

Niels Bohr died in Copenhagen in 1962 at the age of 77. President John F. Kennedy was among those who paid tribute to him for his great contributions.

MAX BORN

Nobel Prize Physics 1954

Max Born was born in Breslau, Germany, now Wroclaw, Poland, in 1882. His father was a professor of anatomy at the University of Breslau and his mother Margarethe, née Kaufmann, came from a prominent Jewish industrialist family.

He received his Ph.D. from the University of Göttingen in 1907. After a short stint in the German army during World War I, he studied and taught at various universities until returning to Göttingen (1921–1933) as a professor. During these fruitful years he worked with many physicists who would become laureates, namely Max Planck, Otto Stern[P], James Franck,* Wolfgang Pauli,* Werner Heisenberg, Enrico Fermi, Paul Dirac, and non-Nobelist J. Robert Oppenheimer.

With the ascendance of Hitler and the promulgation of anti-Jewish laws, Born was expelled from his post at Göttingen and forced to emigrate. In 1933, Born emigrated to England, where he taught at the University of Cambridge. In 1936, he became a professor at the University of Edinburgh, where remained until his retirement in 1953.

He shared the 1954 Nobel Physics Prize with Walther Bothe "for his fundamental research in quantum mechanics, especially for his statistical interpretation of the wave function."

In retirement he returned to Germany, where he died in Göttingen in 1970 at the age of 87.

MARTIN CHALFIE

Nobel Prize Chemistry 2008

American neurobiologist Martin Chalfie was born in Chicago in 1947, son of Eli Chalfie, a guitarist, and his wife Vivian (nee Friedlen), owner of an apparel manufacturing company. His grandparents were immigrants from the Polish-Russian border area.

He graduated from Harvard in 1969 with a B.S. in biochemistry and obtained a Ph.D. degree there in 1977. He moved from Cambridge, Massachusetts, to its namesake, Cambridge, England, to conduct post-doctoral research at the Laboratory of Molecular Biology under Sydney Brenner[M] (Medicine 2002), whom he greatly admired. In 1982 he joined Columbia University's faculty as professor of biological sciences and later became department chairman.

Together with Osamu Shimomura and Roger Tsien, Chalfie was awarded the 2008 Nobel Prize in chemistry "for the discovery and development of green fluorescent protein."

GEORGES CHARPAK

Nobel Prize Chemistry 1992

Georges Charpak was born in 1924 in Dubrovica, Poland, which is now in the Ukraine. When he was seven years old his parents moved to Paris. During World War II he served with the French Resistance and was imprisoned by the Nazi-controlled Vichy government. He was sent to Dachau concentration camp where he survived until liberated by Allied troops. "Luckily I was only regarded as a Pole and a terrorist. They didn't know I was a Jew."[54]

He obtained a B.S. degree from Ecole des Mines in Paris. While studying for his doctorate at the Collège de France, he also worked at CNRS (Centre National de la Recherche Scientifique) under Federic Joliot-Curie (Chemistry 1935). He received his Ph.D. there in nuclear physics in 1954. In 1959 he joined CERN (Central Européen pour la Recherche Nucleaire) and remained there until 1991. He was also a professor at the Ecole Superieure de Physique et Chimie Industrielles in Paris. His strong advocacy of nuclear power likely contributed to France becoming the leading user of nuclear power for electricity.

---

54 Schwarzschild, Bertram. "Nobel Physics Prize Goes to Charpak for Inventing Particle Detectors." *Physics Today* Jan. 1993

Charpak was the sole prizewinner of the Nobel Prize in Chemistry in 1992 for the "invention and development of particle detectors, in particular the multiwire proportional chamber." This allowed measuring the trajectories of particles' mass and electric charge a thousand times faster than before.

He died in Paris in 2010.

GERTY RADNITZ CORI

Nobel Prize Medicine 1947

Gerty Theresa Cori (nee Radnitz) was born in 1896 in Prague, Bohemia, then part of the Austro-Hungarian Empire, now the capital of the Czech Republic. Her parents, Otto Radnitz and Martha Neustadt, were prosperous and well educated. She obtained a doctorate in medicine from the German University of Prague in 1920. There she met Carl Ferdinand Cori, a fellow medical student, also from Prague and also born in 1896. They married in 1920 and became lifelong collaborators, including the research that led to the Nobel Prize.

In 1922 they moved to Buffalo, New York, where they did research at the New York State Institute for the Study of Malignant Diseases. They became U.S. citizens in 1928. In 1931 Carl Cori received an appointment as a professor of pharmacology at Washington University School of Medicine in St. Louis. Initially Gerty Cori could obtain only a low-level position as a research associate, but three years later she was promoted to professor of biochemistry.

Together with Bernardo Houssay, the Coris received the 1947 Nobel Prize in Medicine "for their discovery of the course of the catalytic conversion of glycogen." She was the first female U.S. citizen to win a Nobel Prize in science and only the third woman ever (the first two being Marie Curie and her daughter) to receive the award.

Gerty Cori died in St. Louis, Missouri, in 1957 after a painful ten-year struggle with myeloclerosis. Apart from the usual distinctions received by Nobel prizewinners, a crater on the moon is named for her and the United States issued a postage stamp in her honor.

PAUL EHRLICH

Nobel Prize Medicine 1908

Paul Ehrlich was born in Strehlen, Prussia (now Strzelin, Poland), in 1854 to a prosperous innkeeper, Ismar, and his wife Rosa, née Weigert, both of whom came from families with scientific backgrounds. After attending the universities of Breslau and Strassburg, he completed the requirements for his medical degree at the University of Leipzig in 1878.

Upon graduation, he became head physician at a clinic at the Charité Hospital in Berlin. Ehrlich developed techniques for staining tissues enabling differentiation of blood cells while he was working with Robert Koch (Medicine 1905) who discovered the tuberculosis bacillus. He contracted tuberculosis while performing tests in his laboratory and spent two years recuperating in the dry climate of Egypt. On his return to Berlin, he found out that he had lost his position at Charité Hospital.

He was able to continue his research in immunology and hematology at the Institute of Infectious Diseases in Berlin. Ehrlich collaborated with Emil von Behring (Medicine 1901) in the development of the diphtheria antitoxin. Important as these achievements were, Ehrlich is best remembered for the discovery of the cure for the then scourge of syphilis in 1912 several years after winning the

Nobel Prize. It took 606 trials of compounds to kill the syphilis spirochete he named Salvarsan. Ehrlich came under attack when it was discovered that the medication was not effective when administered in small doses. After further testing for two more years, he developed an improved effective version, Neosalvarsan.

He shared the 1908 Nobel Prize in Medicine with Russian Ilya Metchnikoff* "for their work on the theory of immunity." They were the first Jews to be awarded the Nobel Prize in Medicine.

Paul Ehrlich died in 1915 at the age of 61 in Bad Homburg, Germany. Upon his death Kaiser Wilhelm II, the German Emperor, wrote in a telegram of condolence, "I, along with the entire civilized world, mourn the death of this meritorious researcher for his great service to medical science and suffering humanity; his life's work ensures undying fame and the gratitude of both his contemporaries and posterity."[55] Schools, streets, Deutsche Mark banknotes, and postage stamps were named for him or bore his image. Hitler did away with all these honors, but some were reinstated after World War II.

55 Wile, Frederic William. *Men Around the Kaiser: the Makers of Modern Germany.* Indianapolis, Ind.: Bobbs-Merrill Co., 1914.

ALBERT EINSTEIN

Nobel Prize Physics 1921

Among all the Nobel prizewinners in science, Albert Einstein is undoubtedly the most outstanding and best-known scientist of the twentieth century. Although everyone knows about him, few understand his contributions. His very name has become synonymous with genius.

Einstein was born in Ulm, Wurttemberg, Germany, in 1879 to Hermann Einstein, a salesman and engineer, and his wife Pauline (nee Koch). Both were cultured, non-observant Jews. When he was 17, his parents moved to Italy and then to Switzerland. His scholastic record up to that point was unimpressive. He entered the Swiss Federal Polytechnic in Zurich in 1896 where he studied physics and mathematics. Unable to find a teaching post afterwards, he accepted a position in the Swiss Patent Office. He continued with his education earning a Ph.D. from the University of Zurich in 1905. Four years later he became a professor there and acquired Swiss citizenship.

In 1914, Einstein returned to Germany where he was appointed Director of the Kaiser Wilhelm Institute and professor at the University of Berlin. He was awarded the Nobel Prize in Physics in 1921 "for his services to theoretical physics, and especially for his discovery of the law of photoelectric effect." However, his foremost contributions were in the General Theory of Relativity published in 1915, which brought him international fame. He revolutionized physics by expanding knowledge about the nature of light, time, space, and gravitational influence. His work on mass energy equivalence formula—$E=mc^2$—is well known, whether or not well understood. The 2017 Nobel Prize for Physics was awarded to Barish,* Weiss* and Thorne, who were able to observe gravitational waves predicted by Einstein one hundred years earlier.

With the Nazi's ascendancy in Germany, Einstein's university position was terminated, his property confiscated, his books burned, and his life threatened. Good luck would have it that he was visiting the United States at the time and never returned to Germany. He was invited to join the faculty of Princeton as professor of theoretical physics at the Institute of Advanced Studies. In 1940, he became a U.S. citizen. Due to his great prestige, Einstein was instrumental in influencing President Franklin Roosevelt and the U.S. government to develop the atomic bomb, lest they be preempted by Germany. Ironically Einstein was a pacifist and became a leading voice denouncing nuclear proliferation.

Apart from the numerous honors he received, in 1952 Einstein was offered the presidency of Israel, which he reluctantly declined. He was also a co-founder of Hebrew University in Jerusalem.

Einstein died in Princeton in 1955. His body was cremated. However, his brain was stolen by the pathologist on call, Thomas Harvey, and sliced for further study. Apparently, size does matter: Scientists recently discovered that Einstein's brain has "a colossal corpus callosum." This dense network of neural fibers "is part of what made Einstein's mind so phenomenally creative."[56] Some scientists have debunked this finding.

---

56 Healy, Melissa. "Einstein's Brain a Wonder of Connectedness." *Washington Post* 12 Oct. 2013

GERTRUDE ELION

Nobel Prize Medicine 1988

Biochemist and pharmacologist Gertrude Belle Elion was born in New York City in 1918 to immigrant parents of Lithuanian and Russian origin. She graduated from Hunter College (then a tuition-free women's college, now part of City University of New York) in New York City. Not having the funds to go on to graduate school, she sought a lab job. In her autobiography she noted, "The few positions that existed in laboratories were not available to women... By chance I met a chemist who was looking for a laboratory assistant although he was unable to pay me a salary at the time. I decided that the experience would be worthwhile."[57]

Later she was able to attend New York University where she was the only female to receive an M.S. degree in chemistry in 1941. She did not obtain a Ph.D., instead choosing to work for a drug company. Although corporate scientific jobs were largely closed to women, she later managed to obtain a position with Burroughs Wellcome Research Laboratories and rose to become the head of its Department of Experimental Therapy in 1967, a position she held until 1983. After retiring she served as a

---

57 "Gertrude B. Elion—Biographical." Nobelprize.org

research professor at Duke University. She died in North Carolina in 1999 at the age of 81.

Together with George Hitchings and Sir James Black she received the Nobel Prize in Medicine in 1988 "for their discoveries of important principles of drug treatment." The official statement tells little about her actual contributions. She and her colleagues developed drugs that were effective in boosting the immune response (Imuran) and fighting leukemia (Purinethol), gout (Zyloprim), herpes/shingles (Zovirax), and AIDS (AZT).

She was the first woman elected to the National Inventors Hall of Fame and was the subject of a chapter in Tom Brokaw's bestseller, *The Greatest Generation*.

JOSEPH ERLANGER

Nobel Prize Medicine 1944

Joseph Erlanger was the first U.S.-born Jewish American to win the Nobel Prize in Medicine. He was born in San Francisco in 1874 to Herman Erlanger and Sarah Galinger, who had emigrated from Wurttemberg, Germany. He attended the University of California at Berkeley, where he received a B.S. degree in chemistry, and went on to obtain an M.D. degree from Johns Hopkins in 1899.

In 1906 he was asked to organize the first physiology department at the newly founded medical school of the University of Wisconsin at Madison. Four years later he was appointed head of the Department of Physiology at Washington University in St. Louis. Herbert Gasser,[M] whom he had known at Wisconsin, joined Erlanger at his new post. Their research leading to discoveries relating to "the multiple functional differences of specific nerve fibers" earned them the 1944 Nobel Prize.

Erlanger remained affiliated with Washington University for thirty-five years. He died in St. Louis in 1965.

RICHARD FEYNMAN

Nobel Prize Physics 1965

Richard P. Feynman was born in New York City in 1918. His father, a sales manager for a clothing manufacturer, instilled interest in science early in his son's life. He obtained a B.S. degree from M.I.T. (Massachusetts of Technology) in 1939 and a Ph.D. from Princeton in 1942.

Shortly thereafter, at just twenty-four, he was recruited by the U.S. government to join The Manhattan Project, the group working on the atomic bomb in Los Alamos, New Mexico. Feynman was among those observing the first nuclear bomb test at Alamogordo, New Mexico. After the war, he became a Professor of Theoretical Physics at Cornell University (1945–1950) and then at the California Institute of Technology (1950–1988).

Jointly with Julian Schwinger* and Sin-Itiro Tomonaga, he was awarded the 1965 Nobel Prize for Physics for "fundamental work in quantum electrodynamics, with deep-ploughing consequences for the physics of elementary particles." Feynman was commissioned by NASA's space shuttle program to help investigate the Challenger disaster in 1986. No one had been able to determine the cause of the disaster until Feynman found the answer to this quandary.

Many of his peers considered Feynman a genius, a successor to Einstein. Unlike most scientists, however, he had an idiosyncratic personality. His life was noted for non-conventional, sometimes bizarre behavior. His adventures and foibles are chronicled in his books, *Surely You Are Joking, Mr. Feynman* and *What Do You Care What Other People Think?*, which surprisingly became bestsellers. His life and scientific contributions are chronicled in the biography, *Genius: The Life and Science of Richard Feynman.*[58]

He died in 1988 in Los Angeles.

---

58 Gleick, James. Pantheon Books, New York, NY, 1992.

JAMES FRANCK

Nobel Prize Physics 1925

James Franck was born in Hamburg, Germany, in 1882, to Jacob Franck, a banker, and his wife Rebecca (nee Drucker) who came from a rabbinic family. In 1906, he received his Ph.D. degree from the University of Berlin, where he remained teaching physics from 1911 until 1918. He served in the German Army during World War I and was awarded the Iron Cross for heroism.

After the war he was appointed head of the physics division at the Kaiser Wilhelm Institute in Berlin under Fritz Haber* (Chemistry 1918). From 1920 until his forced exile in 1933, Franck was professor of experimental physics at the University of Göttingen, Germany, which had become an important center of quantum physics. Together with Gustav Hertz[P], he was awarded the 1925 Nobel Prize in Physics "for their discovery of the laws governing the impact of an electron upon an atom."

With ascent of the Nazi regime to power, Franck refused to fire his Jewish co-workers and found positions for all of them abroad. The Franck family themselves fled Germany to Baltimore, Maryland, where he became a professor at Johns Hopkins University. In 1938 he joined the University of Chicago faculty serving as professor of physical chemistry until his retirement in 1956. During the World War II he headed up the university's Metallurgical Laboratory, which was part of the Manhattan Project, although he was an outspoken critic of nuclear weapons.

James Franck died suddenly on a visit to Göttingen in 1964.

WALTER GILBERT

Nobel Prize Chemistry 1980

Walter Gilbert was born in Boston, Massachusetts, in 1932. His father, Richard, was an economist who taught at Harvard University and his mother, Emma Cohen, was a child psychologist who liked to give her children intelligence tests.

He obtained both his bachelor and master degrees in physics and chemistry from Harvard. He then went to England where he received a Ph.D. in mathematics from the University of Cambridge. Gilbert returned to Harvard in 1959 as an assistant professor and, in 1968, was promoted to full professor of biochemistry.

In 1978, while teaching at Harvard, Gilbert showed an entrepreneurial bent when he co-founded Biogen, a leading biotech company, as well as other pharmaceutical enterprises to commercialize some of his discoveries. Starting in 1985 he became involved in the Human Genome Project—a government-funded effort to compile and map the gene sequences in human DNA—which he had long been advocating.

Jointly with Paul Berg and Frederick Sanger, he was awarded the Nobel Prize in Chemistry in 1980 "for their contributions concerning the determination of base sequences in nucleic acids." These findings contributed to breakthroughs in molecular biology and genetic engineering.

VITALY GINZBURG

Nobel Prize Physics 2003

Vitaly Lazarevich Ginzburg was born in Moscow in 1916 to engineer Lazar Efimovich Ginzburg and doctor Augusta Veniaminova, a physicist. He graduated from Moscow State University with a B.S. in 1938 and a Ph.D. physics in 1942. He taught physics at Gorky University (1945–1968) and Moscow Technical Institute (1968–2009).

His career was in jeopardy when he married his second wife Nina Ermakova in 1946. She had been imprisoned on a bogus conviction for plotting an attempt on Stalin's life. Ginzburg might not have been heard of again if he hadn't been assigned to work on the Soviet hydrogen bomb project.

Together with Alexei Abrikosov[P] and Anthony Leggett he was awarded the 2003 Nobel Prize in Physics "for contributions to the theory of superconductors and superfluids."

Ginzburg was outspoken about his views on religion and politics. An avowed atheist, he wrote several books on the subject that got him in trouble with the Russian Orthodox Church. He was a critic of the Russian leader Vladimir Putin whose policies he opposed as a return to totalitarianism.

At the age of 87 he was one of the oldest recipients of a Nobel Prize. Vitaly Ginzburg died in Moscow of cardiac arrest in 2009.

ROY GLAUBER

Nobel Prize Physics 2005

Roy Jay Glauber was born in New York City in 1925. His father was a traveling salesman and his mother an elementary school teacher. He attended the Bronx High School of Science.

When only eighteen years old and a sophomore at Harvard, he was recruited to work on the Manhattan Project that developed the atomic bomb at Los Alamos, New Mexico. He worked on neutron diffusion with such illustrious physicists as Hans Bethe,* Richard Feynman* and Niels Bohr.* After World War II, he returned to Harvard, receiving his bachelor's degree (1946) and Ph.D. (1949), with Julian Schwinger* as his doctoral advisor.

He was awarded the Nobel Prize in Physics in 2005 "for his contribution to the quantum theory of optical coherence," which helps explain how light travels. He received half of the prize money, $650,000, and the other half was shared by J.I. Hall and T.W. Hansch.

In 1956, he received tenure as a physics professor at Harvard, where he spent more than 60 years teaching. Over the years, he received high praise from this students for his teaching ability and personal qualities.

Roy Glauber died in Newton, Massachusetts, in 2018 at the age of 93.

JOSEPH GOLDSTEIN

Nobel Prize Medicine 1985

Joseph Leonard Goldstein was born in Sumter, South Carolina, in 1940 to Isadore Goldstein, a clothing store owner, and his wife, Fannie (nee Alpert).

He received a B.S. (1962) from Washington and Lee University and his M.D. (1966) from the Southwestern Medical School of the University of Texas in Dallas. He was such a brilliant student that he was offered a faculty position there after he completed his studies. While doing his internship at Massachusetts General Hospital in Boston, he met Michael Brown[M] who became a lifelong friend and collaborator.

He spent almost his entire professorial career at the University of Texas Medical School in Dallas where he taught medicine. Before becoming a laureate he had already received fourteen awards for his work.

Goldstein and Brown shared the Nobel Prize in Medicine in 1985 "for their discoveries concerning the regulation of cholesterol metabolism and treatment for the disorders of the blood cholesterol levels." Thereafter, they continued their research together. Their forty years of professional collaboration is the longest scientific partnership in Nobel history.

PAUL GREENGARD

Nobel Prize Medicine 2000

Paul Greengard was born in New York City in 1925, the son of a Jewish vaudeville performer. His mother, Pearl Meister, died giving birth to him. His father remarried shortly thereafter to an Episcopalian woman who brought him up in her faith and prevented contact with his Jewish family.

During World War II he was an electronics technician in the Navy assigned to M.I.T. (Massachusetts Institute of Technology) to develop an early warning system to intercept Japanese kamikaze planes. After the war he attended Hamilton College in upstate New York. He obtained a Ph.D. at Johns Hopkins in 1953 and then traveled to Europe for post-doctoral studies.

His early career included stints with N.I.H. (National Institutes of Health), Geigy Research Labs, Yeshiva University's Albert Einstein College of Medicine, and Vanderbilt University, before settling down as Professor of Pharmacology at Yale University for fifteen years. In 1983 he joined Rockefeller University as Professor of Molecular and Cellular Neuroscience.

Arvid Carlsson, Eric Kandel* and Greengard received the 2000 Nobel Prize in Medicine for their discoveries concerning signal transduction in the nervous system—how the nervous system interacts with neurotransmitters such as dopamine and serotonin.

Greengard used the award money to fund a prize named for the mother he never knew. The Pearl Meister Greengard Prize, which is intended to help promote women in science, is awarded annually to an outstanding woman conducting biomedical research.

He died in Manhattan in 2019 at the age of 93.

FRITZ HABER

Nobel Prize Chemistry 1918

Fritz Haber was born in 1886 in Breslau, Germany (now Wroclaw, Poland), to Siegfried Haber, a prosperous merchant in the chemical business. His mother, Paula, his father's first cousin, died from complications at his birth. Both Haber's parents were non-religious Jews, but he converted to Lutheranism for convenience sake as a young man.

Haber obtained his Ph.D. from the Technical University of Berlin in 1891. Thereafter he worked in the chemical industry and with his father before joining the University of Karlsruhe, where he was named professor in 1906. From 1911 until 1933 he was Director at the prestigious Kaiser Wilhelm Institute in Berlin.

Haber was the sole Nobel Prize winner in Chemistry in 1918 "for the synthesis of ammonia from its elements." His discovery that ammonia could be processed into nitrate that produced artificial fertilizer were a boon to agriculture and hence the world's food supply.

Haber was, however, a controversial figure as the developer of poisonous gases and a proponent of chemical warfare. In World War I, Germany used internationally banned poisonous gases resulting in 150,000 Allied casualties in the battle of Ypres, Belgium. While he was hailed in Germany as a hero, most scientists abhorred his work. His own wife, also a chemist, committed suicide over this matter. Tragically his original cyanide gas formulation of Zyklon was altered by the Nazis and used during the Holocaust in the gas chambers of the extermination camps.

With the advent of the Nazi regime, Haber was instructed to dismiss his Jewish collaborators at the Institute, which he refused to do. In spite of the recognition he received for his services to Germany, Haber felt it necessary to leave in 1933. That same year Chaim Weizmann (the future first President of Israel) offered Haber a directorship position at what became the Weizmann Institute of Technology in Tel Aviv. On his way there he died of heart failure in Basel, Switzerland, in 1934.

ALAN HEEGER

Nobel Prize Physics 2000

Alan Jay Heeger was born in 1936 in Sioux City, Iowa, to a Russian immigrant father, who was a store proprietor, and a U.S.-born mother who was a daughter of Russian Jewish immigrants. His father died when he was only nine and his mother had to move back to Omaha to live with her family.

As the first member of his family to attend college, he went to the University of Nebraska, where he became passionate about science. To further his education, he moved to the University of California at Berkeley to obtain a Ph.D. in Physics (1961) while simultaneously working for Lockheed's Space and Missile Division to help pay for his university education.

After receiving his degree he joined the Physics Department at the University of Pennsylvania where he remained for twenty years. In 1982, he was drawn to the University of California at Santa Barbara by the opportunity to build up a physics department as well as the location. His research there led to the formation of numerous start-up companies.

Heeger, H. Shirakawa and G. MacDiarmid were awarded the 2000 Nobel Prize in Physics "for their discovery and development of conductive polymers." Both of Heeger's sons are scientists—one an M.D. doing immunological research, the other a neuroscientist.

H. ROBERT HORVITZ

Nobel Prize Medicine 2002

Howard Robert Horvitz was born in Chicago in 1947 to a school teacher mother (nee Mary Savitsky) and an accountant father. Both were first generation Americans of Polish/Russian parentage.

He completed his undergraduate studies at M.I.T. (Massachusetts Institute of Technology) where he was president of the student body. He obtained both M.A. and Ph.D. (1974) degrees in biology from Harvard University. He received a post-graduate fellowship for research at the Molecular Laboratory at Cambridge, England.

Since 1974, he has been at the Massachusetts Institute of Technology where he is a professor of biology. He is also an Investigator of cancer biology at the Howard Hughes Medical Institute.

Together with Sydney Brenner[M] and John Sulston—with whom he worked at Cambridge—he was awarded the 2002 Nobel Prize in Medicine for "discoveries concerning genetic regulation of organ development and programmed cell death."

FRANCOIS JACOB

Nobel Prize Medicine 1965

Francois Jacob was born in 1920 in Nancy, France, to Simon Jacob, a merchant, and Therese Jacob, née Franck. His grandfather was a four-star general in the French Army.

He had started studying to become a surgeon when the Germans invaded France in 1940. He fled to England to join the Free French forces under General Charles De Gaulle. A war hero, he received France's highest awards for valor. During the war he suffered severe combat wounds on his hands that kept him from being a surgeon as he had hoped. Consequently he chose a career in science.

After the war he returned to his studies at the University of Paris (the Sorbonne) receiving his M.D. degree in 1947 and his doctorate in science in 1954. He joined the Pasteur Institute where he worked under Andre Lwoff[M] and spent ten years researching the cellular genetics of bacteria. In 1960 he was named the head of the Department of Cellular Genetics, and four years later the Collège de France created a chair in cellular genetics for him.

He shared the 1965 Nobel Prize for Medicine with fellow Frenchmen Andre Lwoff and Jacques Monod "for their discoveries concerning genetic control of enzyme and virus synthesis."

Based on his studies of how traits are inherited, Dr. Jacob believed in the importance of heredity. He was one of four Nobel laureates who were donors to a sperm bank. These Nobelists hoped to demonstrate that their genes were more likely to produce gifted children.

Francois Jacob died in Paris in 2012 at the age of 92.

ERIC KANDEL

Nobel Prize Medicine 2000

Eric Richard Kandel, a neuropsychiatrist, was born in Vienna, Austria, in 1929. His father, Herman Kandel, was born in Galicia (then part of Austro-Hungarian Empire, now Poland) and his mother, Charlotte Zimels, was born in Poland. They went to live in Vienna before their marriage. Though thoroughly assimilated, they were forced to leave Austria after the country was annexed by Germany in 1938. His parents had previously sent Eric and his brother to live with an uncle in Brooklyn and later were able to join them in the United States.

Kandel received a B.A. degree from Harvard and an M.D. degree from New York University Medical School. His interests in the biological basis of the mind led him to earn a degree in psychiatry from Harvard Medical School in 1965.

Starting in 1974 and for the next forty years, Kandel was a professor at Columbia University and at its College of Physicians and Surgeons in the fields of neurobiology, psychiatry, biochemistry and molecular biophysics. As of 1984, he was also associated with Howard Hughes Medical Institute, a leading research organization studying forms of major memory storage.

Together with Arvid Carlsson and Paul Greengard,* Kandel was awarded the Nobel Prize in Medicine in 2000 for "discoveries concerning signal transduction in the nervous system." For the first time the effects of drugs on the brain could be scientifically measured.

PYOTR KAPITSA

Nobel Prize Physics 1978

Pyotr Leonidovich Kapitsa was born in Kronstadt near St. Petersburg, Russia, in 1894. His father was a general in the corps of engineers and his mother, Olga Ieronimovna, née Stebnitsky, was a noted teacher.

He graduated from the Polytechnic Institute of Leningrad in 1918. Kapitsa's schooling coincided with the years of the Russian Revolution, when the name was changed from St. Petersburg to Leningrad. During these turbulent years of civil war, accompanied by famine and epidemics, his young wife and two small children died.

He wanted to study at the University of Cambridge in England, but was not allowed to do so by the revolutionary government. Maxim Gorky, then the most influential Russian author, prevailed on the government to let Kapitsa study abroad. He joined the Cavendish Laboratory at Cambridge, where he received his Ph.D. in 1923 and stayed for thirteen years. In 1934, while he was on a visit to Russia, his exit visa to return to England was cancelled.

After being ardently pursued by the Soviet authorities, he accepted (with conditions) the position as head of the Soviet Academy of Science's new Institute for Physical Problems in 1935. The outspoken Kapitsa was later removed from his post and placed under house arrest for eight years. After Stalin's death he was reinstated, and returned at the Institute for the rest of his life.

Kapitsa shared the 1978 Nobel Prize in Physics with Arno Penzias[P] and Robert Wilson "for his basic inventions and discoveries in the area of low temperature physics."

He never joined the Communist party and his relationship with the Soviet government was always problematic. Nevertheless, due to his great personal prestige he was able to maintain his position while still criticizing the Soviet government. He was actively involved in Russian Jewish causes. Kapitsa was instrumental in the release from prison of fellow Nobelist Lev Landau* (Physics 1962), falsely accused of treason.

Pyotr Kapitsa died in Moscow in 1984.

MARTIN KARPLUS

Nobel Prize Chemistry 2013

Austrian-American theoretical chemist Martin Karplus was born in Vienna in 1930 to a secular Jewish family of distinguished scientists and intellectuals. His father, Heinrich Karplus, was a pathologist and expert in forensic medicine.

After the *Anschluss* with Germany, the family became the target of Nazi-era antisemitism in Austria. He noted that his friends "suddenly refused to have anything to do with me and began taunting me by calling me a dirty Jew."[59] In 1938, the Nazis arrested his father and prevented him from emigrating. After signing over all their possessions to the Nazis, Karaplus, with his mother and brother, Martin, fled to Switzerland and France. They were later reunited with his father before the family sailed to the United States.

Karplus attended Harvard College (A.B. 1950) on a scholarship. He earned a Ph.D. in chemistry at the California Institute of Technology in 1953 under the mentorship of Nobel laureate Linus Pauling. After two years as a postdoctoral fellow at Oxford University in England, he joined the faculty at the University of Illinois and then Columbia University. In 1966 he was named a Professor of Chemistry at Harvard University where he remained

---

59 jewishvirtuallibrary.com

as Professor Emeritus after his retirement. He spent two sabbaticals in France and established a joint research laboratory at the Université de Strasbourg.

Karplus was awarded the 2013 Chemistry Nobel Prize together with Michael Levitt[C] and Arieh Warshal[C] "for the development of multiscale models for complex chemical systems…They developed methods that combine quantum and classical mechanics to calculate the courses of chemical reactions using computers."

J. MICHAEL KOSTERLITZ

Nobel Prize Physics 2016

John Michael Kosterlitz was born in 1943 in Aberdeen, Scotland, to German-Jewish émigrés Hans Walter Kosterlitz, a pioneering biochemist, and Hannah Gresshöner. When the Nazis ordered his father to stop working in a Berlin hospital in 1934, he moved to Scotland where he was offered a position on the University of Aberdeen's faculty. He arranged for his future wife, along with his mother and brother, to join him there. Later in his life the university honored his father by creating the Hans Kosterlitz Centre for Therapeutics.

Michael Kosterlitz received both his Bachelor and Master of Arts from Cambridge and earned his Ph.D. at Oxford in 1969. He did postdoctoral research at the University of Torino in Italy. Thereafter he became a research fellow at the University of Birmingham in England. In 1982, Kosterlitz joined the faculty at Brown University, where he conducted his prizewinning research. He continued there holding an endowed chair in the physics department.

Kosterlitz won the 2016 Physics Nobel Prize with fellow British-born U.S. citizens David J. Thouless and F. Duncan M. Haldane, for "theoretical discoveries of topological phase transitions and topological phases of matter," which laid the foundation for an entire field of theoretical physics.

Kosterlitz, an Alpine climbing enthusiast, has a graded route, *Fessura Kosterlitz* in the Orca Valley of the Italian Alps, named for him.

HANS KREBS

Nobel Prize Medicine 1953

Hans Adolph Krebs was born in Hildesheim, Germany, in 1900, son of Georg Krebs. M.D., a throat surgeon, and his wife Alma Davidson. After graduating from *gymnasium* (high school) he served briefly in the German army.

He studied medicine at the Universities of Göttingen, Freiburg, and Berlin, receiving his M.D. degree from the University of Hamburg in 1925. In 1933, the Nazis terminated his teaching appointment at the University of Freiburg as well as his practice of medicine because he was Jewish. He was fortunate to have been able to move to England on a Rockefeller scholarship.

In 1935 he joined the University of Sheffield as a lecturer. By 1945 he had been promoted to Professor and Director of a Medical Council research unit. In 1954 Krebs joined the University of Oxford as a professor of biochemistry. Sometime later, his research unit was transferred to Oxford.

Krebs and Fritz Lipmann[M] were awarded the Nobel Prize in Medicine in 1953 for the discovery of the urea and citric acid cycles. The citric cycle, often named the "Krebs Cycle" for him, explains how the body converts food into energy. He was knighted "Sir" by Queen Elizabeth II in 1958.

He died in Oxford, England, in 1981 at the age of 81.

HAROLD KROTO

Nobel Prize Chemistry 1996

Harold (Harry) Walter Kroto was born in Wisbech, Cambridge-shire, England in 1939. He was the son of Heinz Krotoschiner and his wife Edith, both of whom were born in Berlin. The family name, of Silesian origin, was simplified to Kroto. Since father was Jewish (though not his mother), it was necessary for his parents to escape from Nazi Germany and find refuge in England. His father was interned in1940 on the Isle of Man as an enemy alien.

Harry Kroto was educated at the University of Sheffield, England, earning a B.S. in Chemistry and a Ph.D. in Molecular Spectro-scopy in 1964. After completing his education he began teaching chemistry at the University of Sussex in England and in 1985 was promoted to full professor. In 2004, he came to the United States and joined the faculty of Florida State University in Tallahassee, Florida.

Kroto won the Nobel Prize in Chemistry in 1996 along with Robert F. Curl, Jr. and Richard E. Smalley for the discovery of C60 a molecule with 60 carbon atoms bonded together in pentagonal/ hexagonal surfaces (also named buckminsterfullerene because of its appearance resembling Fuller's geodesic structure). He was knighted "Sir" by Queen Elizabeth II in 1996.

He was a passionate advocate of science and conducted extensive outreach programs to encourage young scientists. He passed away in Lewes, East Sussex, England, in 2016 at the age of 76.

LEV LANDAU

Nobel Prize Physics 1962

Lev Davidovic Landau was born in Baku, Azerbaijan, then part of the Russian Empire (now the capital of independent Azerbaijan) in 1908, the son of a Russian petroleum engineer working in the oil-producing area and his physician wife.

A child prodigy, he graduated from the University of Leningrad at the age of nineteen in 1927. Thereafter he received a Rockefeller Foundation Fellowship and spent time in several European countries, especially in Denmark with Niels Bohr,* who became his mentor. In 1934 Landau received his doctorate in physical and mathematical sciences from the Soviet Academy of Sciences.

Landau became the head of the Theoretical Department of the Institute for Physical Problems of the Academy of Sciences of the U.S.S.R. in Moscow in 1937. He was simultaneously professor of theoretical physics at the University of Kharkov and Moscow State University. Landau, who despised Stalin's regime, was briefly arrested in 1938 on false charges that he was a German spy (highly unlikely for a Jew). He was released thanks to his colleague Pyotr Kapitsa* who intervened directly with the Kremlin, arguing that Landau's work was too valuable to the state for him to be imprisoned.

He was the sole recipient of the 1962 Nobel Prize in physics "for his pioneering theories for condensed matter, especially liquid helium." At the age of 53, in 1962, the same year that he received the Nobel Prize, Landau was critically injured in an automobile accident in Moscow that prevented him from ever working again. He died in 1968 from lingering consequences of the accident.

KARL LANDSTEINER

Nobel Prize Medicine 1930

Karl Landsteiner was born in Vienna in 1868 to Leopold Landsteiner, a newspaper publisher and journalist, and the former Fanny Hess. Although both parents were Jewish, Landsteiner was a convert to Catholicism. He was so anxious to distance himself from his Jewish background that he brought a lawsuit against the publishers of a Jewish *Who's Who* that included him. Ironically, the resulting notoriety served to publicize what he was so anxious to conceal.

He received his medical degree in 1891 from the University of Vienna and in 1911 he became Professor of Pathological Anatomy there. In 1923 Landsteiner was invited to join the staff of the Rockefeller Institute for Medical Research (now Rockefeller University) in New York City, where he remained the rest of his life. While still working there as Professor Emeritus, he suffered a heart attack in his laboratory and died in 1943.

Landsteiner was the sole honorand of the Nobel Prize in Medicine in 1930. He won the award for his discovery of human blood groups and their use in gauging the compatibility of donor and recipient blood, thereby ushering in safe modern blood transfusion practices. A decade after he received the Nobel Prize, he and his associates described a new factor in human blood, the Rh factor, which was of life-saving importance, especially in obstetrics.

LEON LEDERMAN

Nobel Prize Physics 1988

Leon Lederman, Nobel Prize Physics 1988, receiving the National Medal of Science from President Lyndon Johnson, February 1966

Leon Max Lederman was born in New York City in 1922 to poor immigrant parents who had escaped from Czarist Russia. In his autobiography, he recalled that his father, who operated a hand laundry, venerated learning. Lederman received his undergraduate degree from C.C.N.Y. (City College of New York) in 1943. He spent the following three years in the U.S. Army, obtaining the rank of second lieutenant. Thereafter, he enrolled in the Graduate School of Physics at Columbia University where he received his M.S. (1948) and Ph.D. (1951).

He remained at Columbia as a professor of physics for twenty-eight years, teaching and conducting research. In 1961 he became Director of Nevis Laboratories, a research affiliate of Columbia

University. In 1979 he joined the Fermi National Accelerator Laboratory as Director, supervising the synchrotron, the fastest accelerator in the world at the time. He headed the team at Fermilab that discovered the world of subatomic particles. He joined the faculty of the University of Chicago in 1989 and went on to the Illinois Institute of Technology in 1992, occupying endowed physics chairs at both institutions.

Lederman received the Nobel Prize in Physics in 1988 jointly with his associates Melvin Schwartz[M] and Jack Steinberger* "for the neutrino beam method and the demonstration of the doublet structure of the leptons through the discovery of the muon neutrino (subatomic particle)."

He is the co-author of *The God Particle: The Universe is the Answer, What is the Question?*[60] In 2013 Peter Higgs and Francois Englert[P] were awarded the Nobel Prize in Physics for their work on the elusive particle that came to be named the Higgs boson, also known as the "God particle."

In his later years, he suffered from dementia. His Nobel Prize award money was used to cover his medical expenses. He died in Rexburg, Idaho, in 2018.

---

60 Lederman, Leon M., and Teresi, Dick. *The God Particle: If the Universe Is the Answer, What Is the Question?* Boston: Houghton Mifflin, 1993

ROBERT LEFKOWITZ

Nobel Prize Chemistry 2012

Robert Joseph Lefkowitz was born in the Bronx, New York City, in 1943. His parents, Max and Rose (nee Levine) were U.S. born children of Eastern European Jewish immigrants.

After graduating from Bronx High School of Science he attended Columbia College. He continued at Columbia University's College of Physicians and Surgeons, obtaining an M.D. degree (1966) and graduating at the top of his class. He completed his residency and clinical training at Harvard University's affiliated Massachusetts General Hospital.

Following the completion of his education, he was appointed associate professor at Duke University Medical Center, where he was promoted to full professor in 1977. He is also an investigator at the Howard Hughes Medical Institute.

Lefkowitz shared the 2012 Nobel Prize in Chemistry with Brian Kobilka. "Their research led to the discovery of more than a thousand receptors and ushered in a new era of drug development. Today nearly half of all drugs target G protein-coupled receptors."[61]

---

61 "Nobel Prizes go to alumni Robert Lefkowitz and Alvin Roth." *Columbia University Magazine* Winter 2012–13

RITA LEVI-MONTALCINI

Nobel Prize Medicine 1986

Rita Levi-Montalcini was born in Torino (Turin), Italy, in 1909 to Adamo Levi, an electrical engineer, and Adele Montalcini, a painter. In spite of her father's objections, she enrolled in the University of Torino Medical School, graduating in 1936 with a *summa cum laude* degree in medicine. She earned a further degree for specializing in neurology and psychiatry in 1940.

Mussolini's fascist government's ban of Jews from professions ended her stay at the university. During World War II, she was forced to live in hiding in Florence, where she conducted experiments in a primitive home laboratory. She served as a doctor in refugee camps with the Allied liberation forces.

At the war's end she resumed her academic position at the University of Torino. In 1947 she accepted a short-term invitation from Washington University in St. Louis. She remained associated with the university for the next thirty years. She became a U.S. citizen while retaining her Italian nationality. It was in St. Louis that she made some of her most important contributions. In 1962 she established the Research Center of Neurobiology in Rome, dividing her time between the two institutions.

Rita Levi-Montalcini and colleague Stanley Cohen[M] were awarded the Nobel Prize in Medicine in 1986 for their "discoveries which are of fundamental importance for our understanding of the mechanism which regulate cell and organ growth."

In 2006 Italy honored her by appointing her Senator for life. She was actively engaged in politics in support of liberal causes, which led to personal attacks from the far right. She died in Rome in 2012 at the age of 103, with the distinction of being the longest living person ever to win a Nobel prize.

OTTO LOEWI

Nobel Prize Medicine 1936

Otto Loewi was born in 1873 in Frankfurt Am Main, Germany, to Jakob Loewi, a wealthy wine merchant, and his second wife, Anna Willstatter. He graduated from the medical school of the University of Strassburg in Germany (now Strasbourg, France) in 1896.

Loewi and Sir Henry Dale, an Englishman, were awarded the Nobel Prize in Medicine in 1936, "for their discoveries relating to chemical transmission of nerve impulses." In an early experiment involving frogs, Loewi demonstrated that fluids removed from the heart of one frog and injected in the heart of another resulted in a decreased heart rate in the former and an accelerated heart rate in the latter. He proved that the chemicals released by nerves, rather than the nerves themselves, directly affect the heart.

With the Nazi *Anschluss* (Hitler's takeover of Austria in 1938), Loewi, who had been a professor of pharmacology for thirty-five years at the University of Graz, Austria, was arrested. In exchange for "voluntarily relinquishing" all his possessions, including his Nobel Prize winnings, the Nazis allowed him to leave Austria. After brief stints in Belgium and London, Loewi arrived in New York in 1940. He became a research professor of pharmacology at New York University School of Medicine.

He died in New York City in 1961 at the age of 88.

SALVADOR LURIA

Nobel Prize Medicine 1969

Italian-American Salvador Edward Luria was born in Torino (Turin), Italy in 1912 to Davide and Ester Luria (nee Sacerdote), an influential family with Sephardic roots. He obtained an M.D. degree *summa cum laude* from the University of Torino in 1935. He spent the next three years in the Italian Army as a medical officer.

When it became clear that Mussolini would join Hitler, Luria departed for Paris. When the Germans invaded Paris, he fled by bicycle to Marseille where he was one of the fortunate ones who was granted a visa to enter the United States.

With the aid of his former colleague, physicist Enrico Fermi, Luria obtained a Rockefeller Foundation fellowship at Columbia University. Thereafter, he was a professor of microbiology at the Universities of Indiana (1943–1950) and Chicago (1950–1959). Luria was appointed Professor of Microbiology at M.I.T. (Massachusetts Institute of Technology) in 1959 where he remained until his death in 1991.

Luria shared the 1969 Nobel Prize in Medicine with Max Delbruck and Alfred Hershey for "their discoveries concerning the replication mechanism and the genetic structure of viruses." His research focused on bacteriophages, viruses that attack bacteria, and it helped explain how bacteria develop antibiotic resistance. Curiously, observing the workings of slot machines[62] in a casino led to an analogy of how bacteria behave. One never knows where scientists find their inspiration.

Believing that he should have done more to denounce fascism in Italy, he became politically active in the United States. The outspoken Luria was critical of government military spending, the Korean and Vietnam Wars, which resulted in restrictions on his travel and denial of federal funding for his research. He was dismissed by the University of Indiana because of his role in the University Teachers' Union. However, he moved on to professorships at the University of Chicago and M.I.T.

---

62 Luria, Salvador, *A Slot Machine, A Broken Test Tube: An Autobiography,* New York: Harper & Row, 1984

ILYA METCHNIKOFF

Nobel Prize Medicine 1908

Ilya (Elie) Metchnikoff (also some-times spelled Metchnikov) was born in a village near Kharkov in the Ukraine, then part of the Russian Empire, in 1845. His father was an officer in the Imperial Guard in St. Petersburg married to Emilia Nevak-hovich, who came from a wealthy Jewish family. Metchnikoff was close to his mother and ascribed his love of science to his Jewish heritage. After graduating from the University of Kharkov, he obtained a doctor-ate from the University of St. Petersburg.

In 1908, Metchnikoff and Paul Ehrlich* became the first Jews to win the Nobel Prize in Medicine. Metchnikoff, who worked inde-pendently, was honored for his pioneering research in immunol-ogy. In 1881 he deduced that human blood cells actually function as policing or sanitizing agents, and that bacteria are consumed by devouring cells, which he called phagocytes.

The scientific community of the time violently repudiated Metchnikoff's conclusions, but later, his theories were generally accepted. In 1887 Louis Pasteur himself offered Metchnikoff the directorship of research at his new laboratory in Paris, the Pasteur Institute. After Pasteur's death, Metchnikoff remained in charge of the Institute until his own death twenty-eight years later in 1916 at the age of seventy-one.

Metchnikoff had very definite ideas about living long and well. He advocated the consumption of yogurt to retard the growth of intestinal bacteria, and wrote that alcohol was a great enemy of the human body because it weakens the powers of resistance. He was an early and vociferous supporter within the scientific community of Darwin's theory of evolution.

OTTO MEYERHOF

Nobel Prize Medicine 1922

A naturalized U.S. citizen Otto Meyerhof, was the first American citizen to have won the Nobel Prize in medicine (1922), although at the time he was German. He was born in Hannover, Germany, in 1884 to Felix Meyerhof, a merchant, and his wife, Bettina. He obtained a medical degree from the University of Heidelberg in 1909.

Meyerhof was the first person to apply thermodynamic concepts to the analysis of cell reactions. He shared the Nobel Prize in Medicine in 1922 with Britain's Archibald Hill for "discovery of the fixed relationship between the consumption of oxygen and the metabolism of lactic acid in the muscle."

Concerned by the rise of Nazism, Meyerhof abandoned his post as director of the Kaiser Wilhelm Institute for Medical Research in Heidelberg in 1938. When the Germans invaded Paris in 1940, he fled to southern France, then across the Pyrenees into Spain and from there to the United States. His Nobel colleague Archibald Hill had obtained funds from the Rockefeller Foundation to create a professorship for him at the University of Pennsylvania in Philadelphia, where he remained until his death in 1951.

ALBERT MICHELSON

Nobel Prize Physics 1907

Albert Abraham Michelson has the distinction of being the first American scientist, not just the first Jewish American scientist, to be awarded the Nobel Prize in Physics (1907), and not only that, the first Nobel Prize in any of the sciences—medicine, physics or chemistry.

He was born in 1852 in Strelno, then in the Kingdom of Prussia, now located in Poland. His family immigrated to America when he was only three years old. He was brought up in mining towns where his father was a traveling merchant during the tumultuous era of the California gold rush.

Michelson received an appointment to the U.S. Naval Academy from President Ulysses Grant, graduating as an Ensign in 1873. He remained at the Academy teaching physics and chemistry. Thereafter he took a leave of absence to study in Europe. Michelson is an anomaly in that he did not obtain an advanced university degree.

In 1883 Michelson accepted a position as professor of physics at what is now Case Western Reserve University in Cleveland, Ohio, and later at Clark University in Worcester, Massachusetts. In 1892 the University of Chicago offered him a position to head up its newly formed physics department. At the outbreak of the first

World War, Michelson rejoined the Navy, returning to the University of Chicago thereafter. In 1929 he resigned to work at the Mount Wilson Observatory in Pasadena, California.

He was the sole recipient of the 1907 Nobel Prize in physics "for his optical precision instruments and spectroscopic and meteorological investigations carried out with their aid." His most notable work involved measuring the speed of light. Remarkably some of his findings from more than a hundred years ago are very close to the calculations still in use.

Albert Michelson died in 1931 at the age of 78 in Pasadena, California. All of the universities and institutions with which he was associated named buildings in his honor.

HENRI MOISSAN

Nobel Prize Chemistry 1906

Henri Moissan shown using an electric arc furnace attempting to synthesize diamonds

Henri Moissan was born in Paris in 1852 to an official of a French railroad company and a Jewish mother, Josephine, née Mitel. His formal education was entirely at the University of Paris (Sorbonne). In 1884 he entered the Sorbonne, where he received his *baccalaureate* (B.A.), *licensure* (M.A.) and six years later his doctorate (Ph.D.) in organic chemistry. Thereafter he was able to pursue his research in fluorine compounds thanks to financial support from his wife's family.

He developed and constructed the electric arc furnace, which was instrumental in isolating metals that were considered indissoluble and in developing new compounds. He also attempted to synthesize diamonds using a high-pressure technique, but it resulted only in tiny artificial stones, which came to be named "moissanite."

Moissan was the sole honorand of the Nobel Prize in Chemistry in 1906 "in recognition of the great services rendered by him in his investigation and isolation of the element fluorine, and for the adoption in the service of science of the electric furnace called after him."

Moissan had long been exposed to toxic chemicals (fluorine), which had greatly weakened his health. He died suddenly upon his return to Paris after receiving his award in Stockholm. He was 54 years old.

WOLFGANG PAULI

Nobel Prize Physics 1945

Wolfgang Pauli was born in Vienna, then the capital of the Austro-Hungarian Empire, in 1900. His father, Wolfgang Joseph Pauli (born Wolf Pascheles), a noted physician and University of Vienna professor, was Jewish. His mother, née Bertha Schutz, came from a cultured Viennese family, was Roman Catholic. He was brought up in his mother's religion, but later abandoned the Church.

Pauli obtained his doctorate in physics at the University of Munich in 1928. Thereafter he studied with Max Born* at Göttingen University and Niels Bohr* in Copenhagen. He was appointed professor of theoretical physics at the Federal Institute of Technology in Zurich, Switzerland. From 1935 to the end of World War II, he was a visiting professor at Princeton University, University of Michigan and Purdue University. After the war, he returned to Switzerland to his previous position, which he held until his retirement.

Einstein greatly admired Pauli and nominated him for the Nobel Prize in Physics, which he received in 1945. Pauli was the sole recipient "for the discovery of the exclusion principle also called the Pauli principle." He was a major figure in the development of the quantum theory.

He died in Zurich in 1958 at the age of 58.

ILYA PRIGOGINE

Nobel Prize Chemistry 1977

 Ilya Prigogine was born in Moscow in 1917 just before the Russian Revolution. His father, Roman, was a chemical engineer and his mother, Julia Wichman, was a musician. After the revolution his parents settled in Belgium when Ilya was twelve years old. The family kept a low profile that they were Jewish and survived the German occupation of Belgium in WWII by using false papers provided by the local White Russian community.[63]

Prigogine received both an undergraduate degree and a doctorate (1942) at the Université Libre de Bruxelles and two years later he was appointed chemistry professor there. In 1962 he became Director of the Institute of Physics and Chemistry in Solway, Belgium. In 1967 he was appointed director of the University of Texas at Austin Center for Statistical Mechanics and Thermodynamics, which he founded and was named after him. He divided his time between Austin and Brussels.

Prigogine was the sole honorand of the 1977 Nobel Prize in Chemistry "for his contributions to nonequilibrium thermo-dynamics, particularly theory of dissipative structures."

He died in Brussels in 2003.

---

63 Rice, Stuart Alan. *Special Volume in Memory of Ilya Prigogine*. Hoboken, N.J.: Wiley, 2007

ADAM RIESS

Nobel Prize Physics 2011

Adam Guy Riess was born in Washington, D.C. in 1969 and raised in New Jersey. His father, who had emigrated with his parents from Germany prior to World War II, was a naval engineer and owned a frozen food distribution company. His mother worked as a clinical psychologist.

Riess graduated from M.I.T. (Massachusetts Institute of Technology) in 1992 and four years later received his Ph.D. in astrophysics from Harvard. In 1999 he joined the Space Telescope Science Institute. Since 2005 Riess has been a professor at Johns Hopkins University in Baltimore, Maryland.

Together with Saul Perlmutter[P] and Brian Schmidt, he was awarded the Nobel Prize in Physics in 2011 for "the discovery of the accelerating expansion of the universe through observations of distant supernovae." *The New York Times* wrote a more dramatic version of this description when it announced that the prize was "for discovering that the universe is apparently being blown apart by a mysterious force that cosmologists now call dark energy."[64]

---

64 Overbye, Dennis. "Studies of Universe's Expansion Win Physics Nobel." *The New York Times* 4 Oct. 2011

MICHAEL ROSBASH

Nobel Prize Medicine 2017

Michael Robasah lectures on "The Circadian Rhythm Story" in 2018.

Michael Rosbash was born in 1944 in Kansas City, Missouri, to Alfred and Hilde Rosbash, who fled Germany in 1938. When Michael was two, the family moved to Newton, Massachusetts. His father was a cantor at a local temple and his mother was a cytologist.

Rosbash became interested in biological research at the California Institute of Technology (Caltech), where he received his bachelor degree. After a Fulbright scholarship in Paris, he earned a doctoral degree in biophysics from Massachusetts Institute of Technology (M.I.T.) in 1970. He was a postdoctoral fellow in genetics for three years at the University of Edinburgh in Scotland.

In 1974, he joined the faculty at Brandeis University, where he occupies an endowed chair in neuroscience and conducts research on the brain-neuronal aspects of circadian rhythms. He is also an investigator at the Howard Hughes Medical Institute.

Rosbash won the 2017 Nobel Prize in Medicine with Jeffrey Hall (also at Brandeis) and Michael Young "for discoveries of molecular mechanisms controlling the circadian rhythm." They isolated the gene that regulates the body's daily biological clock. Interestingly, Rosbash noted the importance of using fruit flies in their research, which were also used in the discoveries of many other Nobelists.

RANDY SCHEKMAN

Nobel Prize Medicine 2013

Randy W. Schekman was born in St. Paul, Minnesota. On his paternal side, his grandparents emigrated from Russia, while his maternal grandparents were from Bessarabia (now Moldova), then also part of the Russian Empire. He grew up in a small but tightly knit Jewish community in the Twin Cities.

Schekman graduated with a bachelor's degree from the University of California, Los Angeles (U.C.L.A.), concentrating in molecular biology. In 1975 he received a Ph.D. in biochemistry from Stanford University for his research on DNA replication under Arthur Kornberg.[M] Schekman remained teaching at Stanford and was promoted to full professor in 1994.

In 2013, with Thomas Sudhof and James Rothman[M], Schekman received the Nobel Prize in Medicine, "for the discoveries of machinery regulating vesicle traffic, a major transport system in our cells." Schekman donated $400,000, his share of the Nobel Prize money, to endow a chair in cancer biology at the University of California at Berkeley in honor of his mother and sister, both of whom died of cancer.

JULIAN SCHWINGER

Nobel Prize Physics 1965

Julian Seymour Schwinger was born in New York City in 1918 to Benjamin Schwinger, an apparel manufacturer, and his wife, Belle Rosenfeld. His parents were of Polish background and followed Orthodox Jewish traditions.

A precocious child, young Julian graduated from high school at age fourteen. He then sailed through C.C.N.Y. (City College of New York) where at the age of sixteen he wrote a scientific paper that caught the attention of Isidore Rabi[P], the renown physicist. He arranged for Schwinger to receive a scholarship at Columbia University where he obtained a B.S. and Ph.D. in 1939.

In 1943 he joined the Manhattan Project atomic bomb program and worked on developing microwave radar at M.I.T.'s Radiation Laboratory. After the war he joined the Harvard faculty at the age of twenty-nine, attaining full professorship in 1966. He moved to U.C.L.A. (University of California at Los Angeles) as professor of physics (1972–1994). His doctoral students included future laureates Glauber,* Mottelson[P], Glashow[P], and Kohn[P].

Schwinger, Richard Feynman* and Sin-Itiro Tomonaga shared the 1965 Nobel Prize in physics for "their fundamental work in quantum electrodynamics, with deep-ploughing consequences for the physics of elementary particles."

He died in Los Angeles in 1994 at the age of 76.

EMILIO SEGRÈ

Nobel Prize Physics 1959

Emilio Segrè at the Berkeley Lab,
U.S. Department of Energy, 1954

Italian-American Emilio Gino Segrè was born in Tivoli on the outskirts of Rome in 1906, son of Giuseppe Segrè and Amelia Treves. He studied at the University of Rome earning his doctorate in physics in 1928, mentored by famed physicist Enrico Fermi, a lifelong friend. Segrè wrote a biography of Fermi that was published in 1970.

After a tour of duty in the Italian army, Segrè returned to teach physics at his alma mater. In 1936 he was appointed Chairman of the Physics Department of the University of Palermo. Segrè was on a visit to the University of California's Berkeley Radiation Lab when Mussolini's fascist government passed laws barring Jews from university positions. A longtime opponent of the regime, he decided to remain at Berkeley.

From 1943 to 1946, he was invited to join the highly secretive Manhattan Project in Los Alamos, New Mexico, working on the development of the atomic bomb. Segrè returned to the University of California at Berkeley in 1946 as professor of physics. Except for his time with the Manhattan Project, Segrè was largely associated with the university from 1938 to 1989.

Emilio Segrè shared the 1959 Physics Prize with Owen Chamberlain "for their discovery of the antiproton."

He died in Lafayette, California, in 1989.

JACK STEINBERGER

Nobel Prize Physics 1988

Hans Jacob "Jack" Steinberger was born in Bad Kissingen, Germany, in 1921. His father, Ludwig, was a cantor and his mother, Berta, supplemented the family's income by teaching French and English. The Nazi's rise to power and the accompanying antisemitism prompted his parents to have Jack, then thirteen, and his older brother leave Germany in 1934. They settled in Chicago with foster parents arranged through Jewish charities. The rest of the family joined them in 1938.

Steinberger received a two-year scholarship to the Illinois Institute of Technology. He struggled with menial jobs to pay for the completion of his education and to help support his family. His financial problems were eased when he received a scholarship from the University of Chicago where he obtained a degree in chemistry in 1942. He enlisted in the U.S. Army and was assigned to the Radiation Laboratory at M.I.T. (Massachusetts Institute of Technology). After the war he returned to the University of Chicago with the help of the G.I. Bill and completed his doctorate under Enrico Fermi in 1948.

In 1950 he joined the faculty of Columbia University, which at the time had an extraordinary group of Nobel Prize physicists. In 1968 he left Columbia to take up the position of Director of

CERN (The European Center for Nuclear Research) in Geneva, Switzerland. He officially retired in 1986, but remained actively engaged in advocacy for his areas of interest.

Together with fellow Columbia faculty members, Leon Lederman[*] and Melvin Schwartz[P], he was awarded the 1988 prize in physics "for the neutrino beam method and the demonstration of the doublet structure of the leptons through the discovery of muon neutrino (a subatomic particle)."

HOWARD TEMIN

Nobel Prize 1975

Howard Martin Temin was born in 1934 in Philadelphia to an attorney father, Henry Temin, and his wife, Annette Lehman, an activist in civic affairs. He received his under-graduate education at Swarthmore College in Pennsylvania and later went on to graduate studies in animal virology at the California Institute of Technology in Pasadena. His doctoral dissertation on a sarcoma virus earned him a Ph.D. in 1959.

In 1960, he moved to Madison as Assistant Professor of Oncology at the McArdle Laboratory for Cancer Research at the Medical School of the University of Wisconsin. He rose through the ranks to become full professor of Cancer Research and later of Vital Oncology and Cell Biology. He remained at Wisconsin teaching and doing research for thirty-four years until his death.

Temin shared the 1975 Nobel Prize in Medicine with David Balti-more[M] and Renato Dulbecco "for their discoveries concerning the interaction between tumor viruses and the genetic material of the cell." He believed that cancer is caused by environmental pollut-ants, especially cigarette smoking. Although he never smoked, he died of lung cancer in 1994 at the age of 59.

JOHN VANE

Nobel Prize Medicine 1982

John Robert Vane was born in the town of Tardebigg, Worcestershire, England in 1927. His father, Maurice, the son of Russian-Jewish immigrants, owned a building manufacturing firm. His Christian mother, Frances Fischer, came from a Worcestershire farming family.

Vane received a B.S. degree from the University of Birmingham, England, before earning his Doctorate in Pharmacology from Oxford in 1953. That same year he joined the Department of Pharmacology at Yale University as Assistant Professor.

Two years later he returned to England to work at the Institute of Basic Medical Sciences of the University of London. He remained there for eighteen years. In 1973 he was offered a position as Director of Research with the Wellcome Foundation in London. Some colleagues were critical that he left academia for a commercial enterprise. Vane had no regrets. His research on prostaglandins took place while he was at Wellcome.

Vane shared the 1982 Nobel Prize in Medicine with Sune Bergstrom and Bengt Samuelsson "for their discoveries concerning prostaglandins and related biological active substances." Their research led to the understanding of how aspirin reduces pain and inflammation, and it opened doors to new treatments.

John Vane was knighted "Sir" by Queen Elizabeth II in 1984. He died in Kent, England, in 2004 at the age of 77.

SELMAN WAKSMAN

Nobel Prize Medicine 1952

Selman Abraham Waksman was born in Priluka, near Kiev, Russian Empire (now Ukraine) in 1888. Unlike most Russian-born, Jewish Nobel prizewinners in science, his education and career were not formed in Russia/U.S.S.R., since his parents immigrated to the U.S. when he was only twelve years old.

He received his B.S. degree and his M.S. from Rutgers University in New Jersey. He then went to the University of California at Berkeley where he obtained his Ph.D. in biochemistry in 1918. He returned to Rutgers and spent the next four decades there teaching and doing research as a professor of microbiology. When the university organized the Institute of Microbiology in 1949, Waksman was named its director. He retired from Rutgers in 1958.

He is credited with discovering a number of antibiotics, neomycin and streptomycin (1943) are the best known. There was some controversy about the discovery of streptomycin generated by a lab worker, Albert Schatz, who claimed that he should also have shared in the award. The litigation that followed was settled out of court. The Nobel Prize Foundation determined that Schatz was only a lab assistant working under an eminent scientist and exonerated Waksman. Most of the royalties from the antibiotics benefited Rutgers' Microbiology Institute. Waksman also established a foundation to fund research in microbiology and to underwrite a scholarship fund at Rutgers.

Waksman was the sole honorand of the 1952 Nobel Prize in Medicine, "for his discovery of streptomycin, the first antibiotic effective against tuberculosis." He was hailed and honored throughout the world as a benefactor of mankind.

He died in Hyannis, Massachusetts, in 1973, at the age of 95.

OTTO WARBURG

Nobel Prize Medicine 1931

Otto Heinrich Warburg was born in Freiburg, Germany, in 1883. His father, Emil Warburg, a university physics professor, was descended from Jewish bankers whose business dated back to the sixteenth century. The elder Warburg had converted to Christianity because of disagreements with his conservative Jewish parents. Otto's mother, Elizabeth Gaerther, was Lutheran. Generations of Warburgs had distinguished themselves in science, business, art, and philanthropy. Felix Warburg, from the American branch of the family, was one of the leading figures of American Jewry.[65]

Otto Warburg received a Ph.D. in chemistry from the University of Berlin in 1909. With a view toward seeking a cure for cancer, he obtained a medical degree at the University of Heidelberg in 1911. As a German Army volunteer in the First World War, he rather fancied the military life as a lieutenant in the Horse Guards. However, in 1918, heeding the advice of his father's colleague Albert Einstein, he was persuaded to return to his laboratory. In a letter to him, Einstein wrote: "You are one of the most promising

---

65 The history of the Warburg family in the United States is covered extensively in Stephen Birmingham's bestseller about the German Jewish elite of New York. *Our Crowd: The Great Jewish Families of New York*. New York: Harper & Row, 1967

younger physiologists in Germany . . . can your place out there (in the military) not be taken by any average man?"[66]

Warburg was the sole honorand of the Nobel Prize in Medicine in 1931 "for his discovery of the nature and mode of action of the respiratory enzyme." His pupils included three Nobel Prizewinners—Otto Meyerhof,* Hans Krebs* and Hugo Theorell. Despite his partial Jewish background, Warburg remained in Germany during the Second World War. Though shunned and demoted, he was allowed to continue his research into the causes of cancer. Apparently Hitler had a particular fear of cancer and thought that Warburg's research could lead to a cure. To this end Hermann Goering reclassified Warburg so that at least his life was not in danger.

Warburg was something of a visionary for his times, advocating avoiding cigarette smoking as a means to prevent cancer. He insisted on growing his own food without the use of artificial fertilizers or pesticides, which he believed were secondary causes of cancer. After a career that spanned 65 years and produced some 500 scientific papers, Otto Warburg died in Berlin in 1970.

---

66 Wasson, Tyler, Editor. *Nobel Prize winners: An H.W. Wilson Biographical Dictionary.* New York: H.W. Wilson, 1987

RAINER WEISS

Nobel Prize Physics 2017

Rainer Weiss was born in Berlin, Germany, in 1932. His father, neurological physician Frederick Weiss, was in jeopardy both as a Jew and a Communist. His mother, actress Gertrude Loesner, was Christian. The Nazis abducted his father for testifying against a Nazi doctor for a botched operation. He was released with the help of his wife's politically connected family. The Weiss family fled to Prague.

After the Nazis occupied Czechoslovakia, they were able to emigrate to America with the help of the philanthropic Stix family of St. Louis, who helped them secure visas. The family arrived in New York City in 1939. Rainer earned his B.S. (1955) and Ph.D. (1962) at Massachusetts Institute of Technology (MIT). After postdoctoral research at Princeton, he returned to MIT in 1964 as Professor of Physics.

As a physicist, "Rai" Weiss is best known for his contributions in gravitational physics and cosmic microwave background radiation in astrophysics. Notably, he invented the Laser Interferometric technique basic to the operation of LIGO (Laser Interferometer Gravitational-Wave Observatory), which he worked on for fifty years. LIGO first detected gravitational waves, which are time and space ripples that help scientists explore objects in space. In his theory of probability, Albert Einstein had predicted these findings more than a century earlier. Weiss also co-founded NASA's COBE (Cosmic Background Explorer) satellite program which helps support the Big Bang Theory of the creation of the universe.

Together with Barry Barish* and Kip Thorne, he was awarded the 2018 Nobel Prize in Physics "for decisive contributions to the LIGO detector and the observation of gravitational waves."

RICHARD WILLSTATTER

Nobel Prize Chemistry 1915

Richard Martin Willstatter was born in Karlsruhe, Germany, in 1872 to Max Willstatter, a textile merchant, and his wife, Sophie Ulmann. In 1894 he obtained his B.S. and doctorate on the structure of cocaine plant pigments from the University of Munich where his mentor was Adolph von Baeyer* (Chemistry 1905). To ease the obstacles in Willstatter's professional career, von Baeyer (who had a Jewish mother), encouraged him to be baptized. He did not.

During World War I, he won the Iron Cross for designing gas masks that protected German soldiers from chemical gas in warfare, which ironically was invented by fellow German-Jewish laureate Fritz Haber* (Chemistry 1918). From 1905 to 1911 he was a professor of chemistry at the Swiss Institute of Technology in Zurich, Switzerland. In 1912 he returned to Germany and became a professor at the University of Berlin and a Director of the Kaiser Wilhelm Institute.

He was the sole recipient of the Nobel Prize in Chemistry in 1915 "for his researches on plant pigments, especially chlorophyll." In 1916 he returned to his alma mater, the University of Munich.

When Hitler came to power, Willstatter resigned his post to

protest growing antisemitism despite a show of support from faculty and students. Even though he had offers for positions abroad, Willstatter stayed in Germany. In 1938, the Gestapo came to arrest him, but he tried to escape by rowing across Lake Constance to Switzerland. The Nazis captured him, but through the intervention of the Swiss Ambassador, they later released him to Swiss authorities. He spent the last years of his life writing his biography and died in Muroalto, Switzerland, in 1942.

ROSALYN YALOW

Nobel Prize Medicine 1977

Rosalyn Sussman Yalow was born in New York City in 1921 to immigrant parents with little formal education. At a time when women were largely excluded from careers in science, she was determined to pursue her interest in physics. She was the first woman to graduate with a degree in physics from Hunter College for women (now part of City University of New York). Yalow was the only woman in a class of 400 at the College of Engineering of the University of Illinois at Urbana-Champaign where she received her M.S. in 1942 and a Ph.D. in 1945, both in nuclear physics. She also met her husband while studying there.

The Veterans Administration hospital in the New York City borough of the Bronx hired Dr. Yalow in 1947 as a nuclear physicist in its radioisotope unit. The VA promoted her to posts of increasing responsibility over the years. Later in her career she was a professor at Albert Einstein College of Medicine and Mt. Sinai School of Medicine in New York City.

She received half of the Nobel Prize in Medicine in 1977 (the other half was shared by Roger Guillemin and Andrew Schally) "for the development of radioimmunoassay (RIA) of peptide hormones." This advancement made it possible to measure the concentration of biological substances in body fluids, including insulin in the blood. She was the first U.S.-born woman to receive the Nobel Prize in medicine or science.

Rosalyn Yalow was an exemplary woman who demonstrated to young women of her time that one can be deeply engaged professionally and at the same time be a devoted wife, mother and homemaker—even keeping a kosher kitchen.

She died in 2011 in New York City at the age of 89.

ADA YONATH

Nobel Prize Chemistry 2009

Ada E. Yonath, an Israeli crystallographer, was born in Jerusalem in 1939 into a poor, traditionally religious household with little formal education. Her father, Hillel, a third generation rabbi, and her mother, Esther Lifshitz, were Zionists who emigrated from Lodz, Poland, to Palestine in 1933. Her chronically ill father died when she was only eleven years old, and she had to work at an early age to sustain the family. Poverty did not dampen her intellectual curiosity or her thirst for knowledge.

After completing her compulsory army service in the Israeli Medical Forces, Yonath enrolled in the Hebrew University of Jerusalem, where she received her B.S. and M.Sc. degrees in chemistry and biochemistry. She did her doctoral Ph.D. work at the Weizmann Institute, followed by postdoctoral work at the Mellon Institute in Pennsylvania and at M.I.T. (Massachusetts Institute of Technology). She returned to the Weizmann Institute in 1970 and was promoted to full professor in 1988. Between 1986 and 2004, she simultaneously headed a research unit at the Max Planck Institute in Hamburg, Germany.

Along with Venkatraman Ramakrishnan and Thomas Steitz, Yonath received the Nobel Prize in Chemistry in 2009 for "studies of the structure and function of the ribosome." Her research "unraveled the structure of the ribosome, the cell's protein factory, which synthesizes proteins according to genetic code instructions." She is the first and only Israeli woman to win a Nobel Prize in any field.

Acknowledgments

Throughout the long process of writing the manuscript, Erica Meyer Rauzin, a professional editor, has been helpful with researching and editing the book. She was my constant sounding board.

I would like to extend my appreciation to Gary & Carol Rosenberg of The Book Couple, not only for their work on the book's design, but also for their assistance and advice in so many other ways to prepare the book for publication.

Thanks to Rick Lite for his marketing expertise in promoting the book. He had lived up to his firm's name, Stress Free Book Marketing.

About the Author

Ronald Gerstl has an international background. He was born in Budapest to a Hungarian mother and a father from Curacao, Netherlands West Indies, where he grew up. Along the way he became multilingual in English, Spanish, Dutch, and Papiamentu (the native tongue of Curacao), as well as having knowledge of other languages.

When his family moved to Caracas, Venezuela, Ron went off to New England for his education. He attended prep school at The Taft School in Connecticut and, thereafter, Harvard College, where he received his bachelor's degree. Later he obtained a graduate degree from Columbia University in New York.

He lived in Caracas off and on for some thirty years. His early career experience was in marketing and advertising with leading consumer products companies. Subsequently he founded MAXECON Executive Search Consultants to assist multinational corporations with their executive requirements. He moved to Miami to expand the firm's reach throughout Latin America.

He is married to the former Suzanne Lesh from Indianapolis. Their children, Jennifer and Stephanie, and grandchildren live nearby Palm Beach County. He has travelled extensively, plays lousy golf, and enjoys reading nonfiction. Ron is a geography whiz who rarely misses the answers to questions in related fields on television's *Jeopardy*.

AFTERWORD

Personal Perspectives

I was brought up non-religiously, with little exposure to Judaism and its culture. Although both my parents were Jewish, they were totally indifferent to religion. Neither I, nor my father, nor his father, had a bar mitzvah. However, there never was any question that we were Jewish, and I was well aware of antisemitism. My father's sister's family, who lived in Prague, perished in the gas chambers of Auschwitz.

Many people with whom I have spoken do not seem to comprehend that one can be Jewish and, at the same time, a nonbeliever, agnostic, or atheist. For some, being Jewish is not just a matter of religion. It is just as much about ancestry, ethnic identification, shared experience, and cultural values. Many Jews who are not at all religious are deeply involved in Jewish causes and charities.

"Where are you from?" people often ask. In my case, the answer is somewhat complicated. I was born in Budapest to a Hungarian mother and a father from Curacao in the Netherlands West Indies. Shortly after my birth, my parents returned to their home in Curacao, where I grew up. In my early teens, my parents moved to Caracas, Venezuela, and I went off to school in the United States. I attended a prep school that was quite Episcopalian with daily prayers and hymns and compulsory church attendance on Sundays. That was a marked contrast to my subsequent experience in college at Harvard, where questioning religious doctrine in discussions was common.

While living in Caracas, my numerous cousins and friends were Catholic and I had little exposure to Jewish life. My wife, who is Protestant with deep family roots in Indiana, added further diversification to my life. Living in South Florida, with its large Jewish population, has opened up a wholly different perspective.

My interest and appreciation of the accomplishments and resiliency of the Jewish people came gradually later in life. Reading and observation opened my eyes to their long and painful history. I was enlightened by books such as *My People: The Story of the Jews* by Abba Eban, Howard Sachar's *A History of the Jews in America*, *O Jerusalem* by Larry Collins and Dominique Lapierre, and—on the lighter side—Leon Uris's *Exodus*. Israel's astounding military feats in repelling attacks threatening its very existence, its economic miracle, and becoming a world powerhouse in science and technology cannot but instill pride for both Israel and the Jewish people.

I would like to reach a broad readership with this book, not limited to a Jewish audience. I would like to think that, in a modest way, *The Super Achievers* adds to the awareness of the remarkable contributions Jews have made to mankind.

Selected Bibliography

Books

Birmingham, Stephen. *Our Crowd; the Great Jewish Families of New York* and *The Grandees: America's Sephardic Elite.* Harper & Row, 1969 & 1971.

Brian, Denis. *Genius Talks: Conversations with Nobel Scientists.* Plenum Press, 1995.

Brenner, Lenni. *Jews in American Today.* Lyle Stuart, 1986.

Brenner, Michael. *In Search of Israel: the History of an Idea.* Princeton University Press, 2018.

Collins, Larry, and Dominique Lapierre. *O Jerusalem.* Simon & Schuster, 1972.

Dashefsky, Arnold, and Ira Sheskin, Editors. *American Jewish Year Book 2018.* Springer Nature International Publishing, AG, 2019.

Dershowitz, Alan. *Chutzpah.* Little, Brown, 1991.

Eban, Abba. *My People: The Story of the Jews.* Random House, 1968.

Ehrlich, Judith Ramsey, and Barry J. Rehfeld. *The New Crowd: The Changing of the Jewish Guard On Wall Street.* Little, Brown, 1989.

Encyclopaedia Britannica.

Encyclopedia Judaica.

Gabler, Neal. *An Empire of their Own: How the Jews invented Hollywood.* Crown Publishers, 1988.

Gleick, James. *Genius: The Life and Science of Richard Feynman.* Pantheon, 1992

Goldberg, J.J., Jewish Power. Addison-Wesley, 1996.

Gribetz, Judah. The Timetables of Jewish History. Simon and Schuster, 1993.

Heisenberg, Werner. *Physics and Beyond: Encounters and Conversations,* World Perspectives Series. Harper & Row, 1971.

Herrnstein, Richard J., and Charles A. Murray. *The Bell Curve: Intelligence and Class Structure in American Life.* Free Press, 2010.

Hertzberg, Arthur. *The Jews in America: Four Centuries of an Uneasy Encounter: A History.* Simon and Schuster, 1989.

Heynick, Frank. Jews in Medicine. KATV, 2002.

Isaacson, Walter. *Einstein: His Life and Universe.* Simon & Schuster, 2007.

Itzkoff, Seymour. The Decline of Intelligence in America: A Strategy for Renewal. Praeger: 1994.

Lederman, Leon M., and Dick Teresi. *The God Particle: If the Universe Is the Answer, What Is the Question?* Houghton Mifflin, 1993.

Lyman, Darryl. *Great Jews in Music.* Jonathan David, 1986.

Nadis, Steven J., and Shing-Tung Yau. *A History in Sum: 150 Years of Mathematics at Harvard (1825–1975).* Harvard University Press, 2013.

Pease, Steven L., *The Golden Age of Jewish Achievement.* Deucalion, 2009.

Peterson, Merrill D. *Adams and Jefferson: a Revolutionary Dialogue,* Mercer University Lamar Memorial Lecture Series. University of Georgia Press, 1975.

Prager, Dennis and Joseph Telushkin, *Why the Jews?* Simon & Schuster, 2003.

Reeves, Richard. American Journey. Simon & Schuster, 1982.

Sachar, Howard M. *A History of the Jews in America.* Knopf, 1992.

Schlessinger, Bernard and June Schlessinger. *The Who's Who of Nobel Prizewinners, 1986, Second edition, 1991; Third edition, 1996.* Oryx Press

Senor, Dan, and Saul Singer. *Start-Up Nation.* Twelve/Hachette Book Group, 2009

Sowell, Thomas. *Ethnic America: A History.* Basic Books, 1981.

Uris, Leon. *Exodus.* Doublesay and Company, 1958.

Van Den Haag, Ernest. *The Jewish Mystique.* Stein & Day, 1977.

Viorst, Milton. Sandcastles: The Arabs in Search of the Modern World. Alfred Knopf, 1994.

Wade, Nicholas. *The Nobel Duel: Two Scientists' 21-Year Race to Win the World's Most Coveted Research Prize.* Anchor Press, 1981.

Wasson, Tyler and Gert H. Brieger. *Nobel Prizewinners: An H.W. Wilson Biographical Dictionary.* H.W. Wilson, 1987. *Supplements: Nobel Prize-winners 1987–1996. 1992–1996, 1997–2001*

Wile, Frederic William. *Men Around the Kaiser: the Makers of Modern Germany.* Wentworth Press, 2016.

Zuckerman, Harriet. *Scientific Elite.* Transaction, 1996.

Periodicals

Newspaper articles announcing Nobel prizewinners and their obituaries.

University alumni magazines articles about their Nobel prizewinners.

Internet Sources

Jewish Virtual Library

Jinfo.org

NNDB (Notable Names Database)

Nobelprize.org

Wikipedia

Photo Credits

Cover—Publisher: Swedish Institute, November 2012. Niviere/Sipa, Swedish Institute, November 2012. Reprinted with permission of Sipa Press.

Back cover—Nobel Prize Medal from Stock.Adobe.com.

Alferov, Zhores—Attributed to www.kremlin.ru, copyright expired in nation of origin. Creative commons.

Altman, Sidney—National Institute of Health, U.S. government photograph

Anfinsen, Christian—National Institute of Health, U.S. government photograph

Ashkin, Arthur—With permission of Nokia Corporation and AT&T Archives

Axelrod, Julius—National Institute of Health, U.S. Government photograph

Bacow, Lawrence—property of the author

Baeyer, Adolph von—Public domain, Wikimedia commons

Barany, Robert—National Institute of Health, U.S. government photograph

Barish, Barry—Bengt Nyman, Vaxholm, Sweden, released by photographer to Creative Commons

Baruch Blumberg—Dominic Hart, NASA, U.S. government photograph

Benacerraf, Baruj—National Institute of Health, U.S. government photograph

Bethe, Hans—U.S. Department of Energy, Los Alamos National Laboratory, U.S. government photograph

Beutler, Bruce—Lindau Nobel Laureate Meeting, Lindau, Germany, Patrick Kunkel/Lindau

Bloch, Felix—Used by permission of CERN

Bloch, Konrad—Lindau Nobel Laureates Meeting

Blumberg, Baruch—Dominic Hart (NASA) public domain, U.S. government photograph

Bohr, Niels—AB Lagrelius & Westphal, 1922 Swedish copyright expired, Wikipedia commons

Born, Max—Public domain

Brin, Sergey & Larry Page—Creative Commons

Calvin, Melvin—Lawrence Berkeley National Laboratory, U.S. Department of Energy, U.S. government photograph

Chalfie, Martin—Christian Flemming, Lindau Nobel Laureate Meeting, Lindau, Germany

Charpak, George—Studio Harcourt Paris, 1947; licensed under Creative Commons. Profile Portrait: Lindau Nobel Laureate Meetings, Oct 27, 2015

Cori, Gerty—With Carl Cori, Smithsonian Institution Archives, 1947, U.S. government photograph. Profile: National Library of Medicine, Wikimedia Commons, U.S. government photograph

Curie, Marie—Photograph by Henri Manuel, public domain, circa 1920.

Dirac, Paul—Wikimedia Commons

Einstein, Albert with Robert Oppenheimer—U.S. Government. Defense Threat Reduction Agency, International Communication Agency. Portrait by Sophie Delar, at Princeton in 1935, public domain. Profile: public domain, Bettman Archive, 1931, copyright expired

Ehrlich, Paul—U.S. Library of Congress, U.S. government photograph

Elion, Gertrude—National Cancer Institute, U.S. government photograph

Erlanger, Joseph—Courtesy of the Visual Collections of the Becker Medical Library, Washington University School of Medicine

Englert, Francois and Peter Higgs—By permission of CERN (Image: Maximilien Brice/CERN)

Feynman, Richard—O-ring image by Callum Hackett, shared publicly March 2, 2013. Profile: Creative Commons, copyright Tamiko Thiel

Franck, James—National Archives and Records Administration of the United States, public domain.

Gerstl, Ronald—Property of the author

Gilbert, Walter—U.S. government photograph

Ginzberg, Vitaly—Public domain

Glauber, Roy—Lecture: Christian Fleming/Lindau Nobel Laureate Meetings. Profile: Rose Lincoln/Harvard University; with permission from Harvard Public Affairs & Communications

Goldstein, Joseph—Lindau Nobel Laureate Meetings.

Greengard, Paul—U.S. government photograph

Haber, Fritz—In uniform, copyright expired, public domain. Biography, copyright expired, public domain

Haffkine, Waldemar—Creative Commons, Wellcome Images.

Haroche, Serge—December 2012 by Bengt Nyman, released to Creative Commons

Heeger, Alan—Public domain

Horvitz, Robert—Lindau Nobel Laureate Meetings

Jacob, Francois—Lindau Nobel Laureate Meetings

Kandel, Eric—Bengt Oberger, released to Creative Commons; Profile picture: National Institute of Health, 1978, public domain.

Kapitsa, Pyotr—Public domain. Scanned from "Polska" monthly, August 1964, Warsaw. Photographer Piotr Barącz

Karle, Jerome—U.S. Naval Research Laboratory, U.S. government

Karplus, Martin—Nobel press conference in Stockholm, December 2013, Bengt Nyman, Creative Commons

Kemeny, John—Dartmouth College, Mathematics Department, news service.

Kohn, Walter—Courtesy of the late Walter Kohn. Copyright expired.

Kornberg, Arthur and Roger Kornberg—Linda A. Cicero, with permission of the Stanford News Service

Kosterlitz, J. Michael—Brown University, Creative Commons

Kreb, Hans—1953 copyright expired, public domain

Kroto, Harold—Lindau Nobel Laureate Meetings

Landau, Lev—Public domain

Landsteiner, Karl—Public domain

Lederman, Leon—White House.gov, U.S. Department of Energy, public domain

Lefkowitz, Robert—Bengt Nyman, Creative Commons

Levi-Montalcini, Rita—Courtesy of the Visual Collections of the Becker Medical Library, Washington University School of Medicine: Profile: Wikimedia Commons/Presidenza della Repubblica Italiana

Loewi, Otto—U.S. government photograph created by NASA

Luria, Salvador—U.S. government, public domain

Metchnikoff, Ilya—Copyright expired, 1908, public domain

Meyerhof, Otto—Copyright expired, public domain

Michelson, Albert—U.S. government photograph, U.S. Naval Academy at Annapolis; public domain

Moissan, Henri—United States Library of Congress's Prints & Photographs Division, public domain

Page, Larry & Sergey Brin—Creative Commons

Pauli, Wolfgang—Bettina Katzenstein, ETH Bibliothek, Zurich, Bildarchiv, public domain, Creative Commons

Pincus, Gregory—U.S. Government photograph, National Library of Medicine

Prigogine, Ilya—Public domain

Riess, Adam—MacArthur Foundation

Rosbash, Michael M.—Julia Nimke/Lindau Nobel Laureate Meetings

Salk, Jonas—Wikipedia Commons: University of Pittsburg Archives, published in 1957, Owl student yearbook, copyright not renewed, public domain

Schally, Andrew—Nobel ceremony, courtesy of Dr. Schally. Portrait with author Ronald Gerstl, property of the author

Schekman, Randy W.—UCLA Newsroom

Schwinger, Julian—Smithsonian Institution archives, 1965, U.S. Government; Profile portrait: public domain, Wikipedia Commons

Segrè, Emilio—Donald Cooksey, U.S. Government photograph

Steinberger, Jack—Claudia Marcelloni/CERN, 2008. Courtesy of CERN

Temin, Howard—McArdle Laboratory for Cancer Research, University of Wisconsin Carbone Cancer Center

Vane, John—courtesy of the estate of Sir John Vane.

Waksman, Selman—Donated to the Library of Congress for public use by the New York World-Telegram & Sun, public domain

Warburg, Otto—From 1931, Bundesarchiv, Bild 102-12525 / Georg Pahl / CC-BY-SA 3.0 [CC BY-SA 3.0 de German Federal Archives, donated to the public in 2008. Public domain

Warshel, Arieh—U.S.C. Photo/Mira Zimet, Professor of Chemistry at U.S.C. Dornsife

Weiss, Ranier—U.S. Government photograph

Willstatter, Richard—Copyright expired, public domain

Yallow, Rosalyn—U.S. Information Agency, U.S. Government photograph

Yonath, Ada—University of Kerala, photograph by Hareesh N. Nampoothiri (Haree), NEWNMEDIA. Creative Commons.

Index

Note: Book titles are in *italics*. Page numbers in *italics* indicate photographs.

Summers, Lawrence, 78
Sumter, SC, 57, 176
Superconducting Collider, 141
superconductors, 31, 33, 141, 174
superfluids, 31, 174
supernovae, 31, 216
Swarthmore College, 225
Sweden, 46, 55, 58
Swiss Federal Polytechnic, 163
Swiss Institute of Technology, 234
Switzerland, 45–46, 55, 57, 59–61,
  65–66, 148–149, 163, 189, 214,
  234–235
syphilis, 4, 161
Syria, 50, 74
Szilard, Leo, 68, 69

T
Taiwan, 52
Tangier, Morocco, 51
Tardebigg, England, 61, 226
Technical University of Berlin, 66,
  179
Technion, 127
Tel Aviv, 61
Teller, Edward, 68, 69
Temin, Howard, 15, 29, 61, 225, *225*
Teresi, Dick: *God Particle, The*, 200
Texas A & M, 100
Texas Christian University, 104
Theorell, Hugo, 231
thermodynamics, 36, 209, 215
Thorne, Kip, 20, 141, 164, 233
Thouless, David J., 191
Three Identical Strangers (film), 116
Tivoli, Italy, 221
Tomonaga, Sin-Itiro, 168, 220
topology, 31
Tsien, Roger, 156
Tu, Youyou, 52, 82
tuberculosis, 4, 7, 24, 30, 161, 229

Tunisia, 50, 74
Torino/Turin, Italy, 59, 202, 205
Turkestan, 19, 140
Turkey, 50, 53
Twain, Mark, 1

U
U.S. Census Bureau, 74
U.S. Naval Academy, 47, 210
U.S. Naval Research Laboratory, 96,
  100
U.S.S.R. *See* Russia
Ukraine, 72, 73
Ulm, Germany, 56, 163
Ulysses S. Grant, 210
Union College, 99, 150
Unitarians, 84
United States, 45, 47, 52, 55, 56, 57, 58,
  59, 60, 61, 63, 79, 82, 83, 189, 228
  Jewish émigré scientists, 67, 68, 91
  Jewish population, 73, 74–75,
    119–124
  quota restrictions, 74, 91
universe, expansion of, 31, 216
Université de Strasbourg, 190
Université Libre de Bruxelles, 215
universities, 91–101, 103–104
  barriers to Jewish faculty, 107
  quotas for Jewish students, 93,
    103–104, 107, 121
  presidents of, 107–108
University of Berlin, 63, 91, 98, 139,
  163, 170, 193, 230, 234
University of Birmingham, 191, 226
University of Breslau, 161
University of Buffalo, 100
University of California, Berkeley, 92,
  93, 94, 95, 99, 101, 141, 167, 181,
  219, 222, 228
  endowed chair in cancer biology,
  219